"Macioci's poems lead us on a contemplative walk through the seasons. Closely attuned to nature, they linger on the details of tulip and milkweed, paint vivid images from childhood memories, meditate on impermanence and mortality, aware that "there is no successful way/to study death at a distance." Weeding the garden evokes thoughts of burial. The autumn trees "scribble a signature of loss/teach me how death can be/the origin of perfect beauty". Unsentimental, with the quiet beauty of acceptance, the poems accompany the reader "on the mortal road/of a temporary season."

-Agnes Vojta, author of *A Coracle for Dreams*

"What strikes me the most about *Stoney Seasons* is the organization, how it centers around each season of the year: winter, spring, summer, and autumn, which sounds simple, but is never something I would have thought to do. It is gripping in the way the seasons themselves are as you walk through them, stare out the window at them. And that doesn't really do the book justice in the way the reading does. I wanted to go back and read the entire book again, or just the season I'm in, because I did not think I got everything there was to get even though I read each poem more than once. This is a rare reaction to a book for me, but I think it is something you keep close and open frequently for what it offers."

—Kyle Laws, *The Sea Is Woman,* 2020 Moonstone Press award, *Uncorseted,* Kung Fu Teachery Press, and *Wildwood,* Lummox Press

# STONEY SEASONS

Poems by R. Nikolas Macioci

# Kung Fu Treachery Press

Rancho Cucamonga, CA

Copyright © R. Nikolas Macioci, 2022

First Edition: 1 3 5 7 9 10 8 6 4 2

ISBN: 978-1-958182-11-6

LCCN: 2022940190

Author photo: Sandra Feen

## Acknowledgments:

"Distant Bonfire" / *The Courtship of Winds*

"The Tease of Spring" / *Humana Obscura*

"Snow on the Grass of April" / *Eunoia Review*

"How to Eat Tulips in the Rain"  *Torrid Literature Journal*

"Hummingbird With Folded Wings" / *Torrid Literature Journal*

"The Leaf" / *Torrid Literature Journal*

"Seagulls at McGregar Bay" / *Torrid Literature Journal*

"A Halloween Poem" / *Pink Plastic House*

"The Artist Observes a Dead Tree" / *Sparks of Calliope*

"May" / *The Frogmore Papers  (England)*

"Spring Story" / *The Ravensperch*

# TABLE OF CONTENTS

## WINTER

## SPRING

## SUMMER

# AUTUMN

For Sandra Ditschle, the bravest and most courageous person I've ever known

*"In Ohio seasons are theatrical*
*Each one enters like a prima*
*donna, convinced its*
*performance is the reason the*
*world has people in it."*

-Toni Morrison, *Beloved*

# WINTER

*"Blow, blow, thou winter
wind, thou art not so
unkind as man's
ingratitude."*

--William Shakespeare

*"To appreciate the beauty
of a snowflake it is
necessary to stand out
in the cold"*

--Aristotle

## SMALL TALK IN DEFENSE OF WINTER

It is wrong to call winter the bad guy.
Snow, gray days, early dark, long
evenings pull the mind down into thinking
these things will last forever, despair
become a lifelong companion, but
winter is a vagrant standing at a freeway exit,
begging for approval, not denunciation.

Autumn is the goodbye season, the saddest
season.  Winter affords time to clear
the mind of expectation, welcome shelter
from rundown dreams.

With cozy fire behind wind-rattled windows,
the body sings to someone's surprise
knock at the door, let's in memory
of an ex-lover. Reflections from burning
logs coruscate walls. An old man sits
in his chair by the hearth. He, too, knows
winter, loves it for it's honesty, for the way
it fosters indifference and ragelss resignation.

Gales of snow rip from the sky, later smooth
out under streetlights, each flake a glittering
sliver of mica.  Light of the winter moon,
white as a cotton ball, paints barren trees
silvery black. Winter offers no apology.
If it could speak, it would say "I'm a bitch.
Forsake all other seasons and fall in love with me."

## WITHSTANDING A WINTER NIGHT IN GROVEPORT, OHIO

Opal sky at twilight presages more snowfall.
Wind, on this first day of winter, wallops trees,
whips windows and wrecks wicker chairs
on the front porch I forgot to store.
The streetlamp yawns down flakes slow
as falling asleep, white as a panda's fur.

As I pull away from the nursing home,
I look back at mom's room in the rear view mirror.
Yellowish light brightens her window as if
she were a lone traveler in a passenger car
of a railroad train.

Already, only tire tracks define
the main road, discourage speed over twenty
miles per hour. Ice clumped on the windshield
compacts under wipers, blocks visibility.
It's a drive on the white edge of night,
a high-wire exercise in patience.
Headlights poke through whiteout. I hold tight
to the steering wheel as if to strangle my way home.

I swerve the car onto my road, fishtail a wigwag trail.
House festooned with Christmas lights, bespeak
the battle is over.

Turning into my driveway, I press a button
and the garage door slides upward.
I unbuckle myself from a benumbing ride and
the fatiguing embrace of winter's first storm.

# CANDLELIGHT SERVICE

My friend, Peggy, and I used to attend
candlelight service on Christmas Eve
at The Church of Christ on Reeb Avenue.
Black shadows of gangs and gangsters,
that would one day hang over the South End
like gigantic bats, hadn't arrived yet.
It was a peaceful neighborhood throughout
the 1950s, the kind imagined in movies.

We would hold hymn books, sing
"Oh Little Town of Bethlehem" and
"Joy to the World." Convinced I couldn't sing,
I mumbled words with an extraordinary
off-key resonance.  Peggy sang with perfect
pitch, her uplifted eyes bright as if looking
at the moon.

Songs poured from the congregation.
It seemed singing brought their hearts
out of dusky corners into clear light.

When the minister's sermon ended,
he instructed us to light our candles
from each other.  Dark became a
bright, birthday cake with more than
a hundred flames, a religious chandelier
lit as a grand finale during an upsweep
of belief.

Candles extinguished, We closed our hymnals,
replaced them in the back of pews.

Outside, snow slanted past streetlight.
We brushed off the Oldsmobile's windshield,
covered by immaculate white
like the stripe on a candy cane,
folded into the car, silent and savoring
the afterglow of unanimous contentment.

# TWENTY-TWO-YEAR-OLD TREE SALESMAN

Like bodies wrapped for burial at sea
stacks of bundled fir trees lie on pavement
of the Dairy Queen parking lot. I've a plum,
two-week job between quarters
at The Ohio State University. Pre-Christmas
cold penetrates gloved hands. Numb fingers
fold into fists seeking self-warmth. Light snow,
like white bread crumbs, whips through wind .

When I cut a bundle loose, string snaps open
like a small whip. Grabbing each tree at the top,
I thump its trunk on the ground to unfold
branches. Snow shakes from limbs that loosen
outward like a green dress. I tie each tree
to a temporary fence post, fasten price tags.

Tangy smell of fresh pine surrounds me.
My face beneath a knitted cap burns
from cold, so I step inside the building
for a brief reprieve.

Outside again, a few workers have rallied
around an impromptu fire barrel. Stirred wood
releases sparks bright as minuscule suns.

Throughout the parking lot, people search
for perfect trees, request I twirl them around
for inspection as if I were dancing with them.
I rope purchased trees to roofs of cars.

Sometimes I stuff one into a trunk.
Within two weeks, most trees have disappeared.

Snow deepens. Cleaning commences, and I begin
to miss greeting people. I have always felt alone,
so I know how to react to empty space. Soon,
I'll return to school, and there will be people again,
elsewhere.

CHRISTMAS ILLUSIONS


Though there may be joys this time of year,
I mock the merry heart that leaps into
the holiday, flounders from store to store,
decorates the brain with good intentions.
Strange creature who trims a tree with lights,
wrestles wood into the fireplace, infuses
a house with scent of pine, then falls asleep
watching late afternoon shadows keep him
company. No friends' voices will echo
in a doorway graced by holly garlands.

I should not think of the grave in mid-winter,
but I do.  Only good things are supposed
to matter now. I used to celebrate those
who had grown old, waited for them
to open presents.

Now, I toss another log on silence that lasts
all year, drink and spill wine over tensile,
accept that ice growing down from gutters is
also attached to my life.

Alone by firelight, I think of heaven,
how impractical it is to die
when I am this happy.

## UNDERSTANDING A DECEMBER DEATH

I lift snowy fingers to your face,
cup rejection in my hands. You stare
elsewhere. Distance between us opens
wider. I put my arms around your
unresponsive body, know for sure
your thoughts have fled the room.

One more Christmas I dig into
the trimming box for an ornament
I can hang on the spindly tree you chose
at the last moment from a super market.
Mostly, I want to know why my presents
to you remain unopened. Have you
turned  away from me to someone else?

My feelings for you gleam bright as bulbs
on the tree, colorful blooms of illumination
glow off your cheek before you turn,
start to bed.

I sit alone in a wingback chair. You didn't
linger long enough to repair the brittle end
that seems imminent. If I sleep, I will blame
unwanted darkness for taking away light
I once recognized as love.

## BITTERSWEET

I tramp through foot-high snow
to pick bittersweet, snap off several sprigs
of pea-size crimson berries, carry them home
to decorate the mantle.  I have decided
to forgo a tree and all decorations except
bittersweet.

I arrange a few logs on the hearth,
place kindling, strike a match.
Flames wrap a perpetual embrace around
wood.  Snap of sparks pops echoes
into the otherwise silent room.

I sit in a wingback chair.  Waves of warmth
flash across my face.  I should have said no
even to bittersweet, left my life undecorated.

I'm less complete without your laugh,
our long conversations.  I didn't understand
the fine art of loneliness until I let you go.
My brain wants the sound of someone
coming through the door, anticipation
of hearing someone else's story.

I stir fire, wait for the wind
to come up, for knock of limbs
against the window like the knuckles
of a hand so far from mine.

## ALL THE YEARS OF CHRISTMASES

I grew up eating from a string of old popcorn
out of the trimming box each year. It tasted
as if I were nearing celebration, the surprise
of looking down stairs to see boxes wrapped
in multi-colored paper with ribbons bright
as chunks of rainbow.

As I grew older, I pulled back from
the overkill of Christmas, taught myself
to settle for a darkened room, a wingback chair,
twinkle of tree lights, the taunt of nostalgia.

In memory, traditional Christmases merge.
Very few mark a particular one as unique.
Years have accumulated conformity, the season
lost to predictable routine. I hung the same
blue, aluminum boot on the same limb of
the same tree each year., unpacked and
repacked the same ornaments with the same
anti-climactic feeling as I swept tinsel
from the carpet.

What stands out from year to year is sameness.
Even crackling fire and it's scattered ashes
I have seen before. The same flames filled
the same room with the same emotions.

Grown old, I'm done looking for a special Christmas.
I no longer have the will to examine differences.

# A MEAGER CELEBRATION

I awaken to silence on Christmas morning.
Only the clock ticking, the furnace measuring
out warmth interrupt quiet.

I shower, shave, an actor in a one-character
play who has learned the lines of living alone.
A candy cane in cellophane lies atop
my dresser, the only decoration to denote
a holiday.  I hear my hollow steps in the garage,
heave open the manual door, fold a newspaper
under my arm, and head to the nursing home.

Mom's room is beneath an array of icicle lights
that festoon edges of the roof like electric lace.
Inside the front door, an artificial tree with too
many gold ornaments, too much tinsel reminds
me of a gaudy woman in street-walking garb.

At the nurses' station, a plate of cookies
contains three Christmas trees, two Santa Clauses,
and five stars with butter icing in contrast
to closed double doors farther down the hallway
that signifies someone has died.

Mom's room is next to the closed door.
I enter, wish her a happy holiday, handle her
fragility with fatuous jokes and false mirth.
Like a one-trick magician I perform
hocus pocus to deflect from truth that soon
she will leave me, and I will walk among
winter trees in an orchard of loneliness.

AFTERWARDS

Strings of multicolored lights and decorations,
viewed with anticipation before the holiday,
appear tawdry and senseless now. Before
wreaths appear in windows, trees trimmed,
even the air brims with expectation.

By December's end,  celebration seems like
something borrowed for awhile and gladly
returned. A tangle of tinsel, plastic holly,
trees dragged to curbs comprise the underside
of what for a short time felt sacred.

Stores heap tables with wooden Santas, cedar-
scented candles, and nutcracker soldiers reduced
to the price of candy bars.  Aisle after aisle of fake
pine protrudes from torn boxes.  Broken ornaments
splash reflections from egg-carton-type containers.

What once dazzled, promised meaning, packs
into a trimming box, stored until next year.
The afterwards of Christmas is a garment
turned inside out, showing its threads, jagged
edges, and where the seams are joined.

WINTER LITANY

Winter prevails like a persistent,
unwelcome visitor. Yesterday
it snowed flakes big as torn pieces
of paper, but they didn't stick.
Patches of old snow on the backyard
look nubby as the inside of a white
sweatshirt.  Squirrels nuzzle ground
to find buried acorns. The blotched,
white bird house needs paint.
Downspouts, frozen fountains of ice,
dazzle on rare days when sun slides
through their glass-like surfaces.

Time wanes towards spring, slow
as an hourglass on its side or a canoe
on a creek without current.

Though distance between now
and daffodils dwindles, nothing calms
impatience except the melting away
of months.

In the meantime, a full, January moon
imprints glazed roads with vanilla light,
lengthens lacquered shadows toward
chubby Cupids and foiled hearts.

# THE ABSOLUTE MERCY OF TREES

Look at them, laden in snow,
wearing the Popes's white robes,

In springtime, the woodsman saws
into sap.  Purposeful squirrels claw bark.

What is a tree's salvation? Is it how
it holds sky aloof or how it balances
gold of sun in its branches? The sycamore,
elm, oak have withstood war, resentment.
This is a truth: trees untrouble the earth.

During this winter season,
every limb is open to a critical eye.
Twists, malformations suggest
sculpture.

Chilled wind chews at them, lashes,
sings whistling songs through boughs.

At night they are many-fingered handprints
in the dark that defy visibility.

Look up, see how they trail off
into nothingness.

Soon their juice will rise from frozen soil,
stubborn proof of renewal.

Sudden buds herald spring. Snowdust disappears.
Glimpse first appearance of impatient robins,
trees, a perennial reminder of steadfastness.

# LEARNING TO FORGET IN WELCH'S WOODS

Under a tent of gray sky, a distraction
of geese hangs overhead on the wind
like winter letters to an old lover, cold,
resolute. In a leather jacket with fur collar
I stumble-walk over a stubbled cornfield
across the road from where I live, pass
through a stand of trees, follow a bridle
path, see an occasional rabbit kick up
snow.

On this frigid day, bare limbs tremble
like the bony reach of old people's hands.
It begins to snow again  Flakes whip
across my face.  Bird sounds struggle
through branches as if from a wooden jail.
I see a deer flash boldly out of the brush,
leap into easy disappearance. Who cares

about my quiet solitude, withdrawal
from the sonorous world, that I am alone
in this forest as snow accumulates, covers
my boot prints.

I start home.  Twilight saturates the field.
I keep my hands in my pockets,
arms close to my body,
a mistake ever to have let them hold you.

## WHAT ICE STORMS DO

A vapor light illuminates the night.
From the living room window, I see
the storm wrap everything in cellophane.
Spruce trees sag as if from weight of
sand bags. An invisible aerialist droops
utility wires.  Grass blades are silver spikes.

A car brakes at a stoplight, skids
in a half circle. Few pedestrians risk
uncertainty of footing. One fellow
sacrifices speed for safety, scales down
to half-steps so deliberate each foot
seems anchored by a suction cup.

The icy street shines
like a shellacked tabletop.
When I hesitate from the garage,
bayonet-sharp cold stabs
through my thickest clothing, bare skin
an instant liability.

I salt the sidewalk, sample traction,
trek back inside. The fireplace sizzles logs,
pops sparks orange as tangerine peels.
A compelling calm insulates the house.
I prod a poker into the fireplace, stir
sparks to a greater height, sculpt heat
around wood.  Warmth withers
cold at the window, waylays
the worrisome caress of ice.

## ATTENDING TO SNOW

I didn't need overlapping heart attacks.
I'd had one last December, but I wanted
driveway cleared should I need an ambulance.
I tried snapping fingers, but snow did not
disappear. It was going to be the shovel
and I after all. It stood against the wall
of the garage, having initialed cement floor
with its rusted edge. I didn't want to be
daunted by age.

Garbed for the Arctic, I began plowing
the first strip. Ice-heavy snow gave me
considerable weight to heft. I struck up
a rhythm of shovel, lift, dump, shovel, lift,
dump. Repetition became hypnotic, became
a liturgy of wintertime religion.

Whenever I shovel snow, I think of the house
on Frebis Avenue. There, I took care of Aunt Liz
who had Alzheimer's. She would stand
in the window, watch me clean the whole drive
because she was afraid the phantoms she called
the followers would get me. Since I taught
school and couldn't begin until after supper,
I usually finished in the early dark
when a lamp on a timer would come on,
tint the living room with a warm glow.

Now I live in a house I inherited from parents.
There is no window with anyone standing in it,
waiting for me to finish.

Driveway cleared , I replace the shovel,
stomp feet, remove boots, enter the house.
I live alone, so it's the same quiet that I
always enter into, and the someone
who would greet me is always missing.

## COLD

This winter night goes down as the coldest
I've ever experienced. Even during the 1950
blizzard temperatures had not dropped
this low. I'm reluctant to extend my arm
away from body warmth or to touch anything
in the house that doesn't pulse with blood.
When fingers come into contact with a window,
they feel a freezing shock.

All day I've refilled the hot water bottle,
held it on my lap to keep hands warm.
Lost affections from an unfaithful lover
are not so cold. Even a heavy sweater
doesn't alleviate constant chill.

I'll sit up late, listen to continuous air flow
from the furnace. It's company for a solitary
man.

Weather forecasters predict sun will wash
over tomorrow regardless of sub-zero.

I'm sitting in the kitchen by the register.
When the furnace stops running, silence
underscores desolation.

I shiver for the last time before I pile
extra blankets on the bed, crawl under them,
thinking about dandelion-colored sun
spreading across tomorrow.

## AS A DAY IN WINTER GOES ON

Snow is white as good morals.
I watch wind creep into many faces
of snow, edges shaped by infinity.
Like a hypocrisy, time takes away
permanence of each flake.
Snow lives out its beauty
in nanoseconds, except days when
it accumulates on inclement earth.

In winter I am reminded of death,
gravesides hard as grief
pried open for family, a period
when dying became the norm.
Such thoughts move me
into a desolate melancholy.

As if happiness depended
on the month, I step back from December
to a few months ago when sky blazed
blistering blue, and I did not think
about anything as impermanent as snow.

Shining bits of aluminum
beneath a streetlight, necklaces of snow
lie upon the breast of night.

The streetlight is a hand holding
dark in its palm, showing me how
wind and snow relent, and silence
of white landscape comforts.

Tomorrow morning I will feed juncos
that will peck seeds, shaped like black
teardrops, from ground's frosty crust,
and it will snow again as forecast.
Buddhists would say it is not snowing.
It is the everlasting blossoms of life
falling upon our temporary shoulders.

## SNOW DREAM

A million snowflakes came down.
I counted them. That's how I know.
I felt blessed with the ability to count
snowflakes. What a dream to take up
mileage of my sleep. They were white
as doves accumulated on my shoulders.

After awakening, I wanted the ability to do
something special. My life felt static,
I could go back to teaching, although
I'm like an old book, yellow around the edges.

The whole dream contained nothing but snow,
the affections of snow falling on me
as if flakes were making love .

I'd call it a vivid dream, because it stays
immaculate and perfect in my mind.
The dream has made me want to do
something impossible like inventory
raindrops or kiss the eyelids of a stranger.

I will have to work hard to distance myself
from that dream, from the gift of counting
snow. Something has changed inside me.
I want more miraculous moments. I do not
want to carry this desire inward until I sleep
again. I want the now of everything to count
more, to use up life with rhythms of the blood
crooning a song.

# CERTAIN FACTS ABOUT SNOW

Snow is winter religion, a creed of white
silently worshipped. I honor it
with my eyes, exalt the way it covers
common earth and conventional objects.

In the field behind my house, milkweed
pods fill as if with a dip of vanilla
ice cream, become perfectly colorless
flowers on brown stems.

I grab my shovel, heap, lift, throw.
Walls build with unstoppable height.
I work until I see edges of the driveway.

Finished, I tromp to the garage, slip off boots,
enter the house where logs in a fireplace
spit sparks. I slouch into a wingback chair,
and a spot opens in my heart with desire to share.

I toss another log onto the grate. Orange
sparks fountain up swarms of lightning bugs.
Snapping on a floodlight, I check snow's depth
from a window. It has covered the driveway
again, sparkles like infinitesimal pieces of tinsel.

I settle by the fire, close my eyes, feel nothing
embracing me but snow.

# HAWKS

A hawk rises from a snowy branch,
coils talons, plunges toward a field mouse.
The mouse cannot escape the hawk's grasp.
It is not a long journey to death,
short enough for the mouse to be damned.

The hawk returns, talons empty, knocks snow
dust from another limb. A second hawk alights
in a neighboring tree. Two proud birds
with nothing to do but fall out of snowy sky
and wait for the helpless to give up life.

Snow begins to collect again.
"Come on," the hawks seem to say
"Come out of the cold into our claws."
Their beaks are still as sorrow,
eyes pointed to the ground, hungry.
They clasp sustenance the way people clutch
at love, ravenous to fill what is empty.

All afternoon the hawks hang around,
and all afternoon it snows, lovely hawks
in the lovely snow, and all afternoon
their great wings take them to and from death.

Finally, they disappear,
as does part of the world,
behind an endless curtain of white.

SLED

Snow gleams like slivers of cellophane
under streetlight. I pull my sled
through the intersection of Hinman
and Bruck. A block from home
cars are few at this junction in 1949.
Voices of preteen boys echo down
the otherwise quiet street.

I slam my sled down, press
my eight-year-old chest against wood,
glide through the crossing glazed with ice.
I want to believe my life will remain
this simple.

I stand the sled on end. Snow begins again,
small, white tongues against my face.
I just stand there, cold and questioning
why my father drinks himself into a stupor.
For the first time I'm aware of thinking
about my thinking. Maybe this is what death is,
white winter and unanswering.

I take several more runs, grab the guide bar,
sail forward as if with wings. Even with gloves
my hands are frozen.

A bit weary, I drop away from the other boys,
wrap my neck scarf tighter. Snow thickens.
I trudge down the middle of the street
toward home, baffled by the unknowable.

## THE ILL-FAVORED MAGNIFICENCE OF THE 1950 BLIZZARD

Winter was rough enough to rip moonlight
from the sky. Birds drifted to new lands.
A foot and a half of snow became fashionable.
Rarely did a smooth blue sky swell with sun.
Gravediggers stayed later and worked harder
to open the earth. Dangerous weather reports
danced off men's tongues. The sale of snow
shovels soared.

At nighttime, nothing sparkled in the sky
but a few stars the size of beer caps.
People quit going away from home, afraid
of the truth outside. Ennui spread
in people where there'd never been boredom.
God fulfilled moody fears of the elderly.
Some people let go of everything they believed in.
Rooftops sagged under the weight of early dusk.
Winter chill peeled human skin back to the bone.
Each moment taught a lesson about how to forget
the previous day. "Stay warm! Stay warm!"
Radios shouted. "Renew your faith.
Get on with the skeleton of your day."
Trees and telephone wires sparkled in sheaves
of ice. Amateur survival became a priority.
The earth kept accumulating flake after flake.
There was no expectation of winter mercy,
no way to fight back a world lost in white.

SLED RIDE

I hated to wear galoshes. I thought
them the ugliest thing I could wear,
but snow had accumulated to more
than three feet.  Streets were tunneled
between white canyons. Therefore,
on one of the days that would go down
in history as the 1950 blizzard, I buckled
on the much-disliked boots and clomped
down to the confectionery my parents
owned on Barthman Avenue.

Aunt Betty worked part-time in our store.
She finished work as I entered. Aunt Liz
sat at the counter hiding a beer.  It was illegal
to open one in the confectionery. Dad sold
unopened beer, but many sips were taken
behind the scenes.

Bundled and ready to leave, aunts asked me
if I wanted to go for a sled ride. It was not an offer
a seven-year-old could refuse. They lived a mile
from the store and a block from each other. It was
decided that I would stay all night at one of their
houses. In those days, traffic was minimal.

I grabbed my sled, placed it in the middle
of 6th Street.  Together they pulled me.
It was a famous moment, watching
two aunts I adored bending their backs,

rescuing me for a while from my dad's
heavy drinking that always ended in abuse.
A funny kind of paradise I felt safe in,
as we glided smoothly over a soft, silent,
colorless world.

## MAKING NO SOUND BEYOND THE SPEECH
## OF SUNLIGHT


Sun paws through the window down dining room walls,
a yellow cat stretching its body. I drowse,
curled in a chair, watching it cross the table.
Gloom of winter crumbles within its light.

Years ago, when Mom was alive,
she dozed through afternoons in this sunlit sanctuary,
wore a baseball cap to shade her eyes.

In summer, she rocked in the patio swing,
admired her yard work, a major piece of
identity, but when winter dug into her bones,
she shifted to the bright refuge of the dining room.
There, her peace was prayer-like.

I sometimes huddled in an opposite chair,
hoarding details of her brown-spotted hands,
crinkled eyes, and neck folds. As day shaded to dusk,
she became an old woman in silhouette.

Now, I nap in her chair where cold currents of winter can't
reach me, a place where weeping for what is lost weakens
to blunt memory. Her baseball hat lies in a wicker basket
near my chair like a permanent souvenir.
Outside the window, the world of winter melts,
mauled by the murder instinct of a saffron cat.

## DRIFTED

My sixteen-year-old friends had begun to drive,
Mom said I couldn't drive until
I paid for a car and insurance.
Unable to stand deprivation
any longer, I decided to break the rules.

Several feet of snow lay under mid-afternoon
sun.  My parents owned two cars.
The Oldsmobile had carried them miles away
to shop.  The 1950 Ford, however, stared at me
like a party invitation.  I succumbed,
took keys from my stepdad's drawer
and started the engine.  Thinking I would
stay in their tracks, I backed out ten feet,
slid into the mailbox post.  Acceleration
made rear wheels spin and dig deep holes.
Frantic, I grabbed a shovel from the garage,
like a human backhoe, dug as fast as I could.
Nevertheless, a teenager's antidote in crisis
requires music, so I flung open car doors,
snapped on Tony Perkins singing "Let's Go
on a Moonlight Swim,"and resumed excavating.

I cleared the drive enough to gain traction,
returned the car to the garage, began shoveling
snow to its original state. Defeated,
I trudged into the house, awaited the outcome.

They returned by way of their initial tracks,
stomped into the house and remained quiet.

I learned that day shock has its benefits,
the silent treatment being one of them.

# HUNTING LESSON

Uncle Peck leads me over snowy field stubble
to hunt rabbits. I don't have a gun. I'm just along
to learn about killing. I'm nine-years-old, a city boy
who thinks rabbits are beautiful.

When rabbits scramble from their hiding places,
they make a sound like snow falling against glass.
There is also the sound of their death
when a twenty gauge shotgun with a cylinder choke
bounces a rabbit off its feet.

I follow him, wonder why
I feel revulsion, not excitement.
He carries a gunny sack attached to his belt,
drops each carcass into it.   Blood seeps through,
spots the snow with our trail.

It begins to snow again, the squall dense
as a white bed sheet. Uncle Peck grouches
weather is keeping him from the ultimate kill,
says we are heading home. I try to keep up
behind his footprints.

In the garage, he thumps the blood-soaked sack
onto a workbench, leans his shotgun against a wall
while I watch his face for evidence
of any human emotion.

DIAGNOSIS, 1949

Dr. Guthrie pulls his electrocardiogram machine
up twenty steps to our Barthman Avenue apartment.
Mom is humbled he would make a house call
on short notice and on a snowy day.
I'm in bed with a hundred and three degree fever,
sweating as if I'd been kidnapped.

The doctor wheels his machine into my parents'
bedroom where I've been placed. The equipment
is huge, black and scary with numerous wires
extending from it like the snaky hair of Medusa.
He attaches each contact to my eight-year-old body.
In silence he examines the paper that rolls out of it
like a big, white tongue. I can see the up and down
mountain-like zig zags, the hieroglyphics of health.

A frown creases his forehead, and he steps away
from my bed.  In a low voice he announces
to my mom that I have rheumatic fever.
I don't understand what that means, and delirious,
I barely hear his pronouncement.

I have many dreams about getting out
of bed, but I'm forbidden to do so for three months.
I lie making finger rings from a kit of small beads.
I ask for a toy cash register.  Aunt Ada and Uncle
Heinie bring me one. Many visitors come to peer
at me as if I'm in a casket. They hover around
the bed, go into the kitchen, sit at the table.

Months pass without freedom until one spring day
Mom pauses in my room and tells me I can go
outside. I step onto the porch. Having been confined
so long, it seems as if the world has shrunk.
She takes me for a drive. We roll windows down,
drive through South End streets like two escapees
from solitary confinement. Spring light polishes
everything new: trees, clouds. grass. The whole
afternoon has a hundred birds, all flying free.

# SKATING IN WELCH'S WOODS

From the field I trudge deep into woods,
skates thrown over my shoulder like shoes
with knife blades gleaming moonlight.
I pass tree trunks dark as caves, sentries
guarding the night. An opening leads
into a bright clearing where a frozen pond
excites me to lace on skates.

Earth and sky turn upside down
with each fall, but I persist until
head and feet are numb.

I gather random sticks of wood into a pile,
set them ablaze. Flames soar. A fountain
of fireflies splays upward.

I skate until after midnight. The moon lifts
a little higher. Cutting back through woods
seems darker after firelight. I plod out
of the forest through the field again,
moonlight guiding me home like
a personal beacon.

## COLDNESS

Shrill winds drop temperatures to six
below zero. Moisture at the bottom
of windows, miniature bubble wrap,
measures an inch high.  The furnace
hisses on with only a hint of warmth
to counterbalance chilled floors, walls.
The newscaster warns, "Bundle the kids,
open doors under the sink so pipes
don't freeze."

During the night, threatening winds
whipsaw the house as if it were a
wounded ship on a tumultuous sea.

Ice sculpts the oak tree
in the front yard to a glistening object
of Art, glazes utility wires to appear
insulated in plastic.

The engine of an occasional car echoes
down the icy street as if the driver were
lost from any particular destination.

Tonight, blankets will be piled higher.
Street lamps will shine through pencil
tracings of frost on bedroom windows.
Tonight, cold, an invisible monstrosity,
will clutch the city in its claw
and hold it there like a winter prisoner.

## THE LULL OF LATE FEBRUARY

A furious snow squall,
like a bumbling brute,
reminds that winter does not depart
so fast, but blusters over
first sprouts of daffodils and crocuses

Later,
afternoon reveals blue sky
with stacks of clouds and a hint
of green unfurrowing
on the dogwood tree.

I stand side-by-side
with an early robin
and the hyacinth
breaking through oozy soil.

Soon,
woods will darken
with incipient spring
in each leaf.

It is difficult to see past
the indefinite end
of February
or imagine
myself leaning
against an old rail fence,
letting summer birds create
every possible meaning.

## THE WILL TO WATCH RAIN

Raindrops splat on the windshield,
shrivel, stutter to either side
of wipers, stream into mercury-like
trails, disappear. The wipers continue
to swish and click in metronomic
continuity.

An eighteen wheeler speeds by,
shucks water against my view.
I increase wiper speed that opens a curtain
of vision. Vents spew warm air, allay
the cold melt of March first.

In my driveway, I shut off the engine,
watch rain obscure daylight. A transparent
river washes across glass.
I stare at the scrim of oblivion,
the gulping gush that rushes from gutters.

Granted this may not be the specific
obliteration a friend of mine saw
the day of his suicide. His carbon monoxide
inhalation might have been a major blackout
without stars or a mass of colorful
constellations that could have pulled him
into the vortex. Maybe the only thing he saw
was a windshield full of rain, a watery wall
of sleepy willingness to withdraw behind,
a buildup of drowsy drops one after the other,
one after the other.

## A TRIP TO THE SHED, MARCH 15

A robin does its hop and stop dance
across dormant lawn. A yellow paint daub
of sun shows faint light behind a scrim
of gray clouds.

I slip a key into the cold lock, prop doors
open, see a garden hose that leaked
last summer, a seed spreader caked with
powdery residue. Rusted tools, orange
as sunset, lay cobwebbed upon a built-in
workbench. A capsized can of nails,
a nuisance of neglect, crunch and roll
underfoot.

I'm a bit numb remembering my stepdad
had not finished cleaning before he died.
A faint odor of old wood and stale sunlight
permeate particle board sides. I stand
and stare like a wax figure.
He tired out, broke an arm, had a stroke,
was buried.

I hear birds singing outside as I did
the day he eased away from August
and the taste of the first ripe tomato
from his garden.

I relock the shed, unwilling yet to change
anything, thinking of him in the dark
beneath ground and of the partially wasted
worth of singing birds.

## A BIT OF AN EPIPHANY IN MID-MARCH

Squirrels vandalize the yard, excavate
acorns buried last fall. Their tails twitch,
fan out like plucked ostrich feathers.
Rodent renegades, they scurry up
the dogwood tree, leap to the roof
of the house. Their patter echoes
across shingles.

I amble to the shed, and they scatter
onto utility wires, balanced slackline
walkers.

Inside the shed, air smells of neglect:
garden soil stuck to shovels, tomato
stakes, sun-faded plastic hoses coiled
like green intestines and still retaining
residual water. Cobwebbed chairs and
a table could be props for a Halloween
party. The open toolbox, nails in jars
odds and ends, unswept corners remain
untouched since my stepdad died.
Death taught me to let some things alone.

I palm the shed lock shut, jam hands
into pockets, peer around the yard.
A few squirrels still cavort on wires.
Several, like miniature wrecking machines,
continue to uproot lawn.

I think how lucky these small critters are
to bury something then bring it back
as if it were never gone.

## MARCH LANGUAGE

The beast of March is back today.
Bleak belly of gray sky sags low,
having digested the sun.
Wallops of rain whip windows.

From inside, I watch oak
limbs bounce and bend
with each blast and roar of wind.
The dogwood dances too.

Without a lamp lit, rooms lose
detail, furniture defies definition,
looks like large-boned animals.

I shut the curtains,. Dark captivates
me. It cancels daily concerns, holds
me in a caress of compensation
for what light didn't give.

I exist this way for a while with weary
silence and a slow dream of someone
at the door. Sleepy as I am, I search
night for nothing more than exchange
of syllables, music I seek of another's
arms around my words.

# THE END OF WINTER

Air whitens with flakes.
A curtain of snow stipples
night, an endless scrim
that transforms bushes
and trees into opal mounds.

Billions of lacey stars glitter
under vapor light, I linger
at the living-room window,
wonder if anyone else is
looking out after midnight,
watching the neighborhood
fill up with white like a
a giant cup of powdered milk.

Snow is more than a smooth
nothing. It's a language
with left-over syllables
enunciating spring's delay.

Too much green has broken
through soil to say these
daffodils and dogwood buds
aren't true.

I pull curtains shut, question
why is there no sound as
the world accumulates
crystal flakes, not even

an almost imperceptible fizz
or the shush of feathers
sifting down from a tear
in a gigantic pillow
the god of snow
rests his head upon.

## WHY I STOPPED WRITING

I put my words away like broken toys,
fooled myself into believing what
I wrote mattered.  After twenty-five years,
truth smacked me awake like icy branches
snapping in my face.  I wanted to write
well, but I'm like someone in September
who desired spring when it really wasn't there.

What price have I already paid in search
of perfect language? How often have I
slumped within yellow glow
of a desk lamp while my pen erased
time and space?

I thought it important to see
raindrops on a window as liquid spiders
crawling into oblivion, that someone
cared about seizures of beauty
addicting me to my desk.

Now I let March turn into April
without noticing, let May blossoms open
and linger into October without comment.
Now I glance away from sheets of snow
glazing the yard with glitter from streetlight.
I won't succumb to the twitch of a jay
before it disappears into blue hiding.

I have locked my poems in a drawer.
I no longer take as personal the vacancy
of a park bench or someone in the same booth
every night having dinner for one.

## THE INTERMEDIATE SEASON

From the highway, I see winter expire.
Snow on the ground among forest trees
flickers shadowy sun and hints
of incipient spring.

Steadfast gloom of last week's blizzard
peels away by layers like skins
of a white onion. Along the road,
small clumps of snow, befouled by soot
and eddies of exhaust, are crumpled
paper with smeared black handwriting.

I steer the car South. Chilly birds collect
on utility wires and cables. Flashes
of February light wallpapers the windshield.
I pull down the visor, a hinged shield
that lets me look straight through sunlight
at scattered clouds, puffy white islands
adrift on blue sea.

I'm not fooled thinking I drive towards spring
that teases winter back a bit today.
It's too tidy a transition to be real. I also know
the unthrottled temperament of March can,
like a star pitcher, throw surprise curves.

In the meantime I drive home, tell myself
to untie the tarp from the log pile,
kindle a fire, settle into a wingback chair,
and watch flames tango over the last
cold dances of winter.

## SNOWMAN

Sun melts the snowman's smile. I remove pipe,
hat, buttons. When I built him, I wore driving
gloves inherited from my uncle, smooth black
leather soft as my fingers. The snowman's original
roundness is becoming a watery sheen, firmness
asymmetrical.  What I have taken away contributes
to his ruin.

When I began, I pushed three balls of snow
to perfection, each smaller than its predecessor,
mad to make him handsome, harmless, peaceful,
a man who would dwell on the white lawn
for his short, tenuous life.

The unrepentant sun burns him away,
blends him with silvery, alabaster gloss
on the ground. He cannot withstand an embrace
of warmth that injures, makes him less.
He is becoming water upon which light drifts.
The end must be lamented, sooner or later.

# SPRING

*"It was such a spring day as*
*breathes into a man an ineffable*
*yearning, a painful sweetness, a*
*longing that makes him stand*
*motionless, looking at the leaves*
*or grass, and fling out his arms to*
*embrace he knows not what."*

--John Galsworthy, *The Forsyte Saga*
*(The Forsyte Chronicles, #1-3)*

# APRIL'S TABLE OF CONTENTS

Yellow tulips, cupped hands
with scalloped fingers, open
mouths swallowing sunlight,
swoon in spring breezes.

Blinding blue sky
without a blemish is
an overhead voice
of bickering blackbirds.

A scramble of starlings
swoop down, roam the lawn
like shadowy nomads,
flap wings, flare upward
for a foothold on the birdbath.
Shiny blades of new grass blink
sun, bend under a robin's weight.

Lilacs sweeten the air
as if purple were a scent.

The dogwood tree is a meek
woman in pink sleeves.

Silver light of longer days shimmers
in the apple tree, assures
spring is, indeed, the garment
of winter turned inside out.

## DOCUMENTING DAFFODILS

Daffodils have sprouted
from ground the color of
caramel. They are little
suns on stems, caution lights
in the traffic of spring.
Their asparagus-green stems
are clad in long leaves like
high collars on a thin neck,
not formal wear but the frock
of an established celebrity.
Their fluted heads droop a little
as if to show humility for such
a boasted reputation. When harsh,
harrowing winds hurl in,
their frilly heads shrivel, wilt
to a ghost of themselves.
There is no diva among them.
They are yellow chorus girls
of spring, their brief dance,
a certain waltz away from winter.

## SPRING PREPARATION AFTER A LATE WINTER STORM

Lightning rips gray sky open.  Cracks
of thunder roar from cloud cover like
cosmic criticism.  Ropes of rain slide
down my window like melting icicles.

I look through glass at a distortion
of the dogwood tree, a liquid robin
hopping to a sheltering limb.

I step outside under the porch roof's
overhang, note how rain is restoring
spring, resurrecting buds with lime
touch-up paint.

Rivers in gutters recede. Sun returns,
a shiny, yellow coin.  Its light
brightens waterdrops dripping
pearls of mercury from dogwood
branches.

Tomorrow I will celebrate transition
from winter to days of hope, savor
uncomplicated joy of gathering April
daffodils, a walk in the woods where
I will encounter fragrance of sassafras,
fern and stoke a longing for earthly love.

## MEANDERING INTO MARCH

Streams of gold daffodils,
egg yolks on stems, bonnet
flower beds.  Purple-ribboned hyacinth
press through rutted soil like royalty.
A crocus, the first to depose winter,
dawdles out of the ground
like a fat dowager in yellow hat.
A few patches of snow still blotch lawns,
though increasing warmth inches new grass
through cracks in brick walkways.  Blades
wag in the wind like green, puppy-dog tails.

In the woods across the road
from my house, sun has brought forth hints
of tender buds still tightly wound
in moss and Kelly green cocoons.

I hike through the field into the forest.
Mud sticks to shoe soles.
Without a heavier coat, skin chills,
but the walk cancels claustrophobia
of being walled in since autumn, helps
relieve grievances of winter.

## A NEAR-SPRIING DAY

White cloud mountains scallop
a vault of vibrant blue sky.
Sun, a mystic disc, brightens
mid-march afternoon, melts
remnants of snow.  Slender green
daffodil tendrils slice through soil,
fragile fingers searching for warmth.

Sixty degrees of temperate breezes,
soften winter's previous cold streak.
Thump of a basketball on the neighbor's
driveway, roller blades grinding
the surface attest to the weather change.

I cut an orange in half. Its juice shines
in kitchen light. Its color that of last
autumn's leaves or tonight's sunset.

Sitting on the porch, I study trees
for surface changes, buds on brown
limbs, the beginning of a new branch.
Deep inside myself I am still
a young boy skipping a slice of rock
over rippled creek water, standing
quiet in the middle of woods
to detect bird calls, or trying
to understand why death rambles
into life like an old jalopy and ends it.

## THE TROUBLESOME LOVE OF SPRING

Failure of daffodils
to open delays spring
I know somewhere
nearby, impaired
by insistence
of winter.
A hint of green surfaces
too leisurely
to be taken seriously.
A frozen lake,
a single day of sun,
the rare, misplaced robin
denote an inconsolable
itinerary. Though
the window is without frost,
it's frigid glass imprints
my touch, burgeoning only
blossoms of breath
I breathe onto it.

## OLD LEAVES

It is a short-sleeve or shirtless April day.
Sun has burned off last remnants of winter.
I wince at accumulated leaves left
from last fall, carpeting front yard,
grab a rake from the garage and begin.

Constant motion of pulling the rake
makes me beg for breath. I stop,
stand still, take in more air, realize
years have caught up with me.

I resume raking, aware of inviting
a heart attack not unlike the one
I had two years ago. I don't want to
stop, so I persist at a slower pace.

It's hard to admit I'm at a different
place in life then ten years ago.
Something tells me to quit, but
I remember how easy it was to be
a kid and persevere. I want back
what has been taken from me.

And then I do stop, slump to the garage,
look back at fifteen leaf piles, relegate
bagging to another day.

In the house, I look in the mirror,
see an exhausted face, determined eyes
as if I'd gone to war with aging.

# COUNTING TIME

Smudges of gray-white clouds accumulate.
Strong wind bounces tree branches up and down.
An axe of cold cuts through our heavy coats.
Mom edges her walker toward the car.
A badgering breeze ambushes her balance,
and I grab her arm.

Inside the car,  heater's warm air currents
counteract chill, make her routine doctor's
appointment almost pleasant.

Halfway there, we pass through upscale
neighborhoods where houses with
floor-to-ceiling windows collect sun
like glass buckets. The houses invite
speculation about their inhabitants
the way grab bags entice guessing.
I imagine someone relaxing in a club chair,
watching a sunspot brighten the room.

I brake in the parking lot, pull the trunk release.
It pops open like a soda can. I bring Mom's walker
around to her door, help her stand. All the while,
I'm aware of the limited sand in her life's
hourglass  sensitive to her struggle to navigate
with a bone-on-bone hip joint.

We enter the doctor's office, seat ourselves.
Light from South and West Windows whitewash
walls, distract for a moment from monotonous cold
of late March and the immanence of mom's decline.

## THE TEASE OF SPRING

The label of winter still sticks to each day
like a tagged warning to forestall
the anticipation of spring.

Cold spells, like inescapable hands,
grip the dogwood's new growth.
Lacerating, March winds lash green
hints of the tree's buds.

A forecast of snow clears store shelves,
bread and milk suddenly priceless.

By morning, streets and yards thicken
six inches.  Deep white appears fastidious,
otherworldly, a mask hiding faces
of hyacinths, minuscule tendrils
of daffodils.

At best, these mid-days of March lack
the brazen force of February, bring
a hint of green to grasses.

Tomorrow, crews will plow, spew
moon-colored streets into the air
in an explosion of silvery flakes,
clear the way for the meek emergence
of March's demise.

## ON THE EDGE OF APRIL

Snow squalls look obsolescent now,
a winter outlaw galloping into spring.
Black clouds occlude the sun like
cosmic cataracts.

I lift a heavy coat from the closet,
wrap a wool scarf around my neck.
For a moment, I vacillate about whether
to venture outside or stay within.
In the foyer, however, I find myself
opening the door.

The cemetery is three blocks away,
past Christ's flower shop, Norm's
Market, and the Methodist Church.
Cold kills pleasure of a casual walk,
shifts me into tighter steps.

At the gate I look across acres of
lives memorialized in marble.
I climb the knoll to my dad's marker,
a brown plaque trimmed in gold for
an army vet. Snow begins to fall
a little thicker, a white vandal obscuring
names.

I turn back toward the road leading in,
I feel I can't leave before silence
of sympathy clears away offensive loss,
not before camouflage of snow fills up
this forest of stones.

## TULIPS

Every spring, cousins, Butch and Jim,
and I raised Brownie cameras
to preteen eyes to freeze still shots
of the Tulip bed.

Aunt Mary, for no reason we understood,
had mounded the plants.  Hence,
we called it the Tulip Hill.

Each spring, we pooled our money,
saved to buy black and white film.
Color was a nugget of gold,
too expensive for our meager pockets.

All through late March, we watched
that mound for earth's green fingers
to punch through soil.  I believe
we would hear them break ground.

Finally, we saw cup-like flowers.
As if in church, we knelt on that hill
to snap holy moments. It didn't matter
that our pictures weren't color. We had seen
the color, captured nearness of barefoot weather
and summer vacation.

Later, after receiving our snapshots
from the mailman, we compared pictures,
stored them in special shoeboxes

decorated with decals collected
from inside cereal cartons.  We slept easy
that night, having immortalized memories
in magnificent monochrome.

## PINE CONES

Winter has left its signature behind
in the form of pine cones strewed
across the yard like a lumpy carpet.

It's three days before April,
not warm enough for t-shirts.
Light jackets are in order.
I open the garage door,
drag a rake to the back
of the house, glide tines over
lawn as if casting a line
into open water, drag
in a rakeful of pine cones.

My stepdad used to do this
monotonous job, Mom too.
Memories linger from loss.
I see them raking pile after pile,
clearing the yard to an immaculate
spring green.

I have no wife. I have no children.
The weight of this labor is mine
alone.  I pull the rake toward me,
bend, thrust it out again.  Over
and over I repeat an act of getting,
letting go until all these corpses
of winter are accounted for.

I see sprouts of peonies green
as a parrot's wing protruding
from the soil, signs of new life
poised in their pointed tips.

## BIRTHDAY SOLO

The saxophone seduces the air
like soft sobs of a soldier.
I slouch in the cafe's corner
with a scotch and water, watch
a couple seclude themselves in dance.
She succeeds in sculpting herself
to his silhouette. They take little,
slide steps, look asleep, shadowed
into one another by the absence
of direct light.  Their closeness
insinuates mutual desire.

It's my birthday, and I feel
especially old sitting here so stiff,
somewhat formal in a jacket and tie.

It's clear the time is past for me
to exchange mutual looks, to slip
hands together in a new friendship.

The couple stops dancing, stands still
for several seconds before leaving
the floor as if to say the dance was
unnecessary for them to stand this close.

I study the space where they were,
submerging in drink the urge
to walk onto the dance floor
and embrace an imaginary partner.

The saxophonist takes a break.
I'm surrounded by strident screeches,
sputter of small talk. I shove my empty
glass aside, stray outside
where night is huckleberry black
and candleless.

## UNENCUMBERED BIRTHDAY

Clouds are white pillowcases
on a blue clothesline of sky.
Wind badgers dogwood branches,
bounces them a little. I lift
my coat from a hook, pull it on.
First day of April is a blustery
bid for better weather.

I amble along a wooded path,
sun, a gold balloon, does not
warm brisk chill. Today is my
birthday, and I want something
more than cake and candles.
Whispering creek water,
hidden birds' scattered trills
neutralize encroachment
of age: eyes and brow lined,
lips thinned, hands wrinkled
as if wearing skin a size-too-big.

I meander among trees, see blooms
and buds have slipped into spring
like little secrets.

After hours of hiking, I turn toward
home, plod from woods to a freshly
plowed field. Clumps of black soil
stick to my shoes. I stop, look back.

The forest appears dark as the inside
of a fist, a place where internal
shafts of light clothed me with a sense
of being held, a special mantle worn
in lieu of the swagger of celebration.

# SPRING STORY

Black as licorice, starlings peck through tufts of grass,
while squirrels skidder over lengthening shadows,
ramsack the yard for last year's acorns. A stray robin
hops, stops, hops, stops. How quietly they go about
their business of knowing exactly where to find food.
It's almost a comedy to watch these creatures cavort
among themselves without running into each other.
They do not provoke, as we do, worlds of trouble.
They parade the yard like ambassadors of April.
At the end of the yard, near rusty, chain-link fence,
peonies poke an inch from hard, brown soil.
A nameless, random weed invades burning bushes
on the property line.  New growth reveals it's hiding
place from which it will be plucked come warmer days.

I watch these details from behind the dining room
window as the neighbor's cat creeps into the picture.
I know it's mission among birds all too well.
It's slack tail and slinking paws prowl toward the back
of the shed and disappear. I think about the short time
each creature has, and how its life is made of chance.
I could, if needed, chase the cat to save the birds.
It would be distressing to see a bird caught
in fuzzy jaws. At such a time, I feel omnipotent,
the power fall into my lap, that, right or wrong,
could stymie nature's hunger.

## WEEDING ON THE FIRST WARM DAY OF APRIL

Last year's Primrose stems, brittle and thin,
overshadow this year's new growth, green
as arugula. I fold to a kneeling pad,
fit hands into work gloves, curl fingers
around spring-loaded clippers. Scissor-like
blades, sharp as piranha teeth, cut
a handful of stems, a miniature corn shock.
I pitch clippings into the waste barrel,
yank out wild grass, shake off loose soil,
level it again.

This close to ground, I think of burial,
wonder if other people, when working
soil, think of how close they are to
what someday will cover them.
I shift a palmful of dirt from one hand
to another, imagine how dark six feet
under would be.

Finished weeding, I stand back, see green
spread before me like a blanket of shamrocks
burnished by sunlight that stays forever
above the Earth.

# SURROUNDED BY APRIL

It is a perfect yellow day, a ten
on spring's scale. Tender leaves unfurl
on every limb of every tree. Windless,
cloudless, blue sky unscratched by jet exhaust
canopies arugula-green lawns.
I ache for a way to express appreciation
for beauty of a day that brings me to a standstill.

In Schiller Park, couples hold hands, stroll
beneath blossoms, appear to close distance
between expectation and desire.

I'm sitting on a bench in late afternoon.
Ducks on the pond maneuver for bread
offered by passersby. I want to say to these
same passersby, how lucky to have someone
to hold, because this perfect spring day
is not a time to be alone.

I drove to this park to see people mingle,
to hope someone special might amble into my life.
Unnoticed, I'll simply feed the ducks,
walk back to my car as the sun drops
into shadow like a broken lamp.

## AN APRIL STORM

Distant thunder growls. Its echo lingers
several seconds. The guttural sound rolls
out of darkness. I've lit a single lamp.
Night is a one-dimensional nothing
against the window in which I see my
reflection. Rain drips into my kitchen
where raccoons have torn away shingles.
An occasional squall slams the window.
Another blast of rain roars against the roof.
Otherwise, it's silent except for the sound
of the refrigerator repeating its cycle and
the hum of a distant plane cutting through
a chaos of clouds.

It's 10:30, and I'm too awake to sleep,
I'm sitting in a straight-back chair as if
waiting for someone who likes poetry
and writing to walk into the room, sit
down beside me, and begin the most
compelling conversation I've ever had.

It's started to rain again. Wind-driven
gusts pound glass underscored by lightning
flashes and more thunder than a Baptist preacher.
The storm retains its heft for another twenty
minutes during which I learn a thousand things
about loneliness, about begging someone
to alleviate solitude that claws my heart.

## SNOW ON THE GRASS OF APRIL

The first days of unpredictable April turns its
sack of tricks upside down, empties its contents
of cold winds and a smattering of snow flakes,
small enough to have fallen from a giant
salt shaker, upon the village of Dedham.
It's spring's sleight of hand powdering lawns
with remnants of winter that disappear in seconds,
a reminder not to pencil in warm weather too soon.
Nevertheless, a hint of cloud-white blossoms
has surfaced on magnolia trees, and shoots
of hyacinths have pushed through hard soil.

I think twice about days by a steady fire,
windows frosted with lacy designs,
the dogwood bowed in gowns of ice.
I don't know if I'm ready to be released
from winter's raw embrace, its remembered rap
of wind on the windows and how it held me
cloistered in long nights and early lamplight.
During winter, I mellowed into solitude.
Now, it is a kind of loss to account for as
sun brightens creeks and streams, and branches
puff out pink blooms.

Another April I live alone, become a hound pulling
at his leash of isolation, longing for a pairing
of the heart.

SURPRISE TULIPS

Twenty tulips the color of yellow Jasper
christen spring, jabber with pedal tongues
when a breeze blows across them.
I call them surprise tulips because each year
I forget they are on the east side of the house
until I discover them while mowing.

This year, I photographed them from beneath
on a diagonal, achieving a regal look.
I enhanced them by applying numerous filters.
The finished shot appears to be brushed
with the stain of tea and the blue of a Siamese
cat's eyes.  Tulips transformed
into lovely ladies in waiting

EASTER, 1973

Rain rockets down. A rampage
of thunder follows. Rush
of water creates rapids along curbs,
floods streets. Local parks cancel
outdoor egg hunts. Across the field,
at the Lutheran church, ladies
in pretty hats linger in cars, then,
under a sky of umbrellas, lunge
en mass for the door, sanctity of
Sunday drenched as more cars drive
into the lot.

I've lit a lamp because outside light
grows dim as a candle at low wick.
Weather doesn't wind down. Claws
of lightning rip clouds, radiates them
with blinding flashes. As rain pummels
the roof, I prefer a more pleasant
mood at the movies.

I race from car to shelter
of the marquee, pay for my ticket,
take a seat. The theater is half full,
the dark a blend of deep gray and
flickering light flashes from the screen.
I do not think I have offended the day
by being here. My hands are folded
in my lap as if to offer a prayer
to celluloid for salvation.

## OLD EASTERS

It's been years since I received an Easter
basket with real eggs dyed in primary
colors and nested in plastic straw,
a chocolate bunny centered in the midst
of dozens of jelly beans.

I was young, yearned for easy candy,
not for a day of convenient grace
when people bowed heads to
resurrect faith.

Much like the Tooth Fairy, the Easter
Bunny delivered while I was  asleep.
Wrapped in bright, yellow cellophane,
the basket reminded me of a sunny day.
Many treats waited  behind it's gloss.

On those mornings, though excited,
I was reluctant to tear the basket apart.
I always found a fold I could slip
my hand through without ruining
the cellophane. When I finally did
remove the whole piece, I'd look
through it at a window, and everything
outside reflected an amber glow
as if the whole world had changed from
one in which I lived as an abused child
to one of temporary escape.

## SUNSPOT

Much of my life has been spent finding
a sunspot on hardwood floor in mid-afternoon.
Something about a sunspot settles my mind.
It is a supreme message of contentment,
hope coming through a window in the winter
when everything is frozen, yellowish light
impossible to look at and not want it there
forever. It is a quiet gift eyes grab and hold
as if it were someone loved whose warmth
I don't want to let go of.

While on appointments, I have watched it
coming through a window in the waiting room,
seen it on the seat beside me while driving.
It soothes when I become skeptical of life.
I would never pull curtains shut on it, but
as sun drifts west to its daily death, dark
becomes the norm again.   Until then,
I want to be mesmerized by the sun's buttery look,
not look away from where it has gathered
all of my sadness into one daffodil-colored
melancholic place.

## THE ANATOMY OF FAITH

Faith is
an ambiguous,
tedious
undertaking,
allowing pretense
of knowledge,
infrequent facts,
blind management
of feelings.
It's a game
of guess,
letting imagination
make truth from hope.

Faith is
thinking
an empty room is filled
with what you believe
needs to be in it:
a spiritual fireplace,
comfort of divine furniture,
a window with light
of early spring
blazing through it.

Faith is
bankrolling the unknown,
paying out of the pocket
for unanswered questions.

## RECITATION

When the room slightly tilts,
I'm afternoon drunk on poetry.
I read aloud as if I were in a hospital
room consoling a patient. Even though
I have no audience,  I enunciate, sculpt
syllables, give this gift to myself .
Even without a taste of vodka gimlet,
I am alive with stanzas, lines, words
that embroider meaning onto the cloth
of my mind.

It is an afternoon of coconut-white clouds,
daffodil colored sun, a day without
the faintest hint of predicted rain.
April squirrels supervise the yard,
as I utter Prufrock and Millay.
My voice resonates, fills the room
and hollows of the hallway.
I read until my voice is not my own,
but the one I lend to loneliness.

As a boy, I walked among wild
flowers, through woods, reciting Frost,
apprehensive such solitude might become
a habit, elegant language a mercy
for the moment.

# THE ETERNAL MONOLOGUE

I know the language of lost souls
whose whispers I hear
throughout the cemetery. I know
what they talk about: pastures of sun
that will not warm them again,
burning orange and red hills
of autumn along rural roads,
waking to spring morning's silver light,
watching bluish pink twilight slide
down behind a stand of trees.

I intercept their messages
that merge with millions of clouds
and mesh with the murmur of wind.

I stand near the iron entrance gate,
its rusted hinge, a tiny voice between me
and those once here. They have control
of this territory and say as much
in early daffodils, in pink and purple
ribboned hyacinths,

and in the vivid touch of clear moonlight
that validates the supremacy
of each monument.

## ANTITETICAL SPRING

I give up the blossoming trees of May.
I have one outside the window within
hands reach, a dogwood with a few
panther-black branches that winter ended
the life of.

I give up daffodils too, the cliche of spring,
yellow imitations of the sun.

I give up walking out the door in a light
sweater, shamefully indifferent to the chill.

I give up cleaning flower beds squirrels tore up
when they buried acorns in the fall.

I give up the twitter of birds that awaken me
in the morning like feathery alarm clocks.

I give up standing beneath an umbrella when
sun streaks a downpour and everything outside
is made of rain.

I give up tulips, hollow hand--painted tea cups
balanced on green stems.

I give up early, vanilla snow that surrounds
a purple hyacinth.

I give up crocus, allium, iris.
I give up all that I want because I was told
everything would come back to me
when I love again.

## HOW TO EAT TULIPS IN THE RAIN

First, accumulate necessary items:
a rain slicker, knife, fork, and plate.

Scissor off a half dozen fresh tulips.
Cut stems into small pieces. Full length
protrudes, feels as if you have a mouth
full of green spaghetti. Petals, however,
like slippery slugs, slide down the gullet
with gag-free ease. Immediately, you
will savor exotic flavor. Whether
you let them marinate on the tongue
or swallow them right away is a matter
of personal taste.

Finally, for an assist at digestion,
open your mouth to dripping clouds.

By now, you will have experienced
one of nature's finest, gourmet secrets.

A word of caution. Consult your doctor
before pursuing this recipe.
Tulips eaten by men have been known
to cause excessive gas, pregnancy, and
the growth of posterior bouquets.

It's rewarding to expand your culinary
repertoire with new delicacies. Next time
I'll talk about delight of ingesting daffodils.

## MEMORIAL DAY VISIT TO THE CEMETARY

Mom and I stand among tombstones,
discolored teeth, each leaving a tooth mark
on mortality.  An enormous eighty-year-old
oak shades us, its leaves, anchored skiffs, buoy
on an occasional breeze. Staring at acres
of death, I think death is a business
perfect as a polished coin.  It buys us,
offers no refund.

Mom uses a cane.  A walker would be better
but would dent her vanity. She is ninety-three,
diminished to ninety-six pounds. I prefer
to remember a younger Mom with a strong
resemblance to Hedy Lamarr, or
a thirty-year-old wiping the kitchen sink top
to perfection.

We've been told my cousin's remains were
disposed of behind my grandparent's monument.
We hunt, guessing at anything resembling ashes.
We find nothing.

I tip my head back as far as it will go to see
the oak collecting sky, blue as an emperor butterfly.
I look around at divots where soil settled
in pockets and indentations on interments.
I wait as if for some form of science fiction
to reassemble dust of the dead.

At this moment the privilege of returning home
seems delicate as the oriole
balanced at the top of the oak.

## MAY

Blossoms are burning in the blowing sun.
Crows shriek wild songs. In the backyard,
an amazement of thin green leaves inch out
of dogwood branches. Early robins, orange
breasted, pull worms from their sleep. I
carry the ceramic birdbath from the shed.
Later, I listen to the hiss of water
from the uncoiling hose. All around me
things are opening. The beginning of
abundance grows out of the earth. There's
gladness in the body. It seems worthwhile
to live even without love. My shoulders
blaze with warmth as I bend to gather twigs
from silky grass. I glance at clouds, infinite
pillows of the sky. Plump rose buds, along
the back of the house, unfurl a little each day.
Life is more difficult for me in the spring.
I sleep with a window open, arms empty
of another person. I don't want to hurry
back to the loneliness that started
in the morning and still calls my name. I
want to sleep, not caring how I could have
lived differently.

# SUMMER

*The summer sun was not meant*
*for boys like me.  Boys like me*
*belonged to the rain*

--Benjamin Alire Saenz , *Aristotle*
*and Dante Discover the Secrets*
*of the Universe, #1*

## NUDGED TOWARD NEUTRALIZATION ON
## A FRIDAY NIGHT

It is summer.  Insects bat their bodies
against windows. I'm writing this draft
to renounce the scalding loss of love.
It's not just another poem concerning sweat
running off an arduous effort to keep
a relationship. It's a draft depicting
ethereal aftermath, abounding elegance
that accompanies an end.  Like
satisfaction from walking in surf
along desolate beach, there's something
soothing about rescuing self from
what was once desired.

Bugs keep knocking against glass.
What do they want? Light? To relocate?
Lord knows. If I let one in, it will lurch
at the desk lamp, lock itself into
a repetitive cycle of going nowhere,
an act of futility much like a connection
to someone with no substance.

I snap off the lamp, bugs go wherever
bugs go in the dark.  I see my way
down half-lit hallway, rough draft I leave
on my desk an reenactment of recovery.

# SIGNIFICANCE OF A DAY IN JUNE

We sit on the swing. It's a sunny day.
Mom thinks the birdbath needs filled.
I unwind the tangled hose, drag it
like a stubborn mule. I set the nozzle
to spray and submerge it until
streams spill over the rim like liquid tinsel.

Back on the swing, I see an absence
in Mom's eyes. Her deteriorated hip
precludes doing much outdoor work.
I assure her there are still simple tasks
she can handle.

I help her up. She uses a small, favorite
spade as a cane. She says she wants it
buried with her to substantiate
the hard-working life she's known.
At the corner of the patio, she chops
weeds from a flower bed, her movements
slow as sunset, precise as acupuncture.
When she finishes, she shuffles back
to the swing, avoids imbalance by plopping
down hard. The swing slams
against the back of the house, and I joke
that velocity almost threw me off.

Settled, she reminisces about yardwork
she's done. "I'm so glad I planted those
burning bushes. They make a perfect barrier."

We keep swinging, lifting feet from ground
with every glide. "I planted that Rose of Sharon.
Look how big its gotten. I've done a lot of work
in this yard, have everything just the way I want it"

A murmuration of starlings assault
the bird bath, interrupt her words. It's
impossible for the whole flock to drink at once.
Six dive at the water only to be flapped away
by the next onslaught. At one point, five birds
appear to be choreographed, three on the rim,
two suspended in flight like black corsages
pinned to the air, then the birds disappear
as if they'd never been there.

Mom becomes weary, wants to go
into the house. I help her up. She uses
one of my arms as the other cane.
Once she is inside, I return to the swing,
but the rhythm isn't the same.
The empty space seems to grow emptier
with every push of my feet.

I miss our casual conversation, her hyper
attentiveness to detail, the almost constant
advice she gives as if to guarantee
I'll have a good life.

I swing a little longer, try to imagine living
without her, know there is no successful way
to study death at a distance.

I stop swinging, place the hose nozzle back
in the birdbath to replace water
raucous birds have splashed out.
I know those same starlings will never return.
They were only passing through, but the gift of
their beautiful, mid-air dance turns loss
into a perfect memory.

## DANDELIONS AND GRIEF

Dandelions, yellow dowsing rods,
turn toward the sun.  Grief, gray as gravel,
takes me away from where I want to be.
Brahms, nightingales, mourning doves
make sounds of grief. Dandelions give
wine, salad and grow old fast. They raise
their heads against summer's first blue sky.
Grief scuttles across the face of religion,
scarring rituals of belief, settles in
Cassandra's eyes where there is nothing
but doubt. In a field, corn-colored dandelions
catch fire from orbiting day, decay to a seeded
fuzzball that breeze catches in its net, and seeds fall
to earth like stars. Grief paints walls of the heart
with pain. If grief had knees, it would fall down
on them, beg to be noticed. Dandelion seeds
tear from stems, drift in air, miniature parachutes.
In the hand, they disintegrate like ash, delicate
as anonymity.

I once saw a young boy take a bouquet
of dandelions to a grave. He placed
them at the bottom of the tombstone.
I was sitting several yards away on a bench,
heard words that could have been a prayer
or a scream of insanity over loss. I saw
his surprise when I went to the pump
and brought him a bucketful of water
for his flowers. He thanked me, called me mister.

Beyond that, we didn't talk. I started
toward my car, turned back and noticed
the dandelions, in spite of the water,
had already begun to wilt. The last thing
I saw from my car was the boy
smashing his fist against the tombstone.

## FOURTH OF JULY POEM

Tumbling stars slide from the sky.
Fierce rockets rip upward.  A blue
umbrella of sparks spreads open
like an exploding planet.  Pieces
float to the ground, dissolve.
A Roman candle erupts, shoots flaming,
multicolored orbs into the dark.
The purple peony crackles overhead.
The scarlet chrysanthemum's trails fade.
I watch this display from above
churchyard trees in my backyard.

In another direction, at a greater distance,
muffled thunder of fireworks
resonates like something known
but out of reach.

I'm patient with a single life, but
on a night of celebration like this,
yes, there are moments when I look around
to see who is near.

FIREWORKS

Sky crackles and crumbles.
My car, parked along a side road, reflects
explosions of light. I perch on the hood,
think how fire fascinates, the irresistible
burn of color trailing back to earth.

The common peony shell, marshmallow white,
spreads open, melts to invisibility. A horse tale
firework streams out like a woman's long hair
in a fast-moving convertible. The finale
forges a polychromatic sky.

I think of James Wright who used the word
"alone," and its variations, often in his poetry.
Like an animal or an old man going away
to die, I slump alone on this back road.

I pull from the berm. It's almost midnight.
I drive for another hour with no idea
of which road to follow next.

## AT THE MERCY OF BASEBALL

I panicked at Camp Saint Joseph
when recreation time rolled around,
hid behind one of the cottages,
got caught for sneaking away
from sports I hated. I was an
eight-year-old no one had ever
explained the rules to.

I didn't want to humble myself
in front of boys my own age.
I would have gouged a jugular
rather than ask for help.
Past a certain age, a boy just doesn't
do that.

I discovered another hiding place.
Behind an enormous oak, about
fifty yards from the diamond,
I would lean back against the tree,
fantasize that someday I would be
exempt from the embarrassment
of baseball.

One afternoon, a camp counselor
caught me with my eyes shut, ordered
me out to the field. At bat, I doodled
my foot in the dust, swung. Strikeouts

brought me to the bench. I prayed
for this time of torture to be over,
for a little of this Italian boy's self-esteem
to be preserved.

## A SPIRITUAL BURST OF BEING AT SUNDOWN

Sunset pushes dark toward dawn.
In last hours of light, fireflies burn
like memories of my youth, corn-yellow
glow a miniscule miracle. I watch dusk
plunge yard into deep-green shadows.

A mourning dove coos it's doleful sound,
a song for the heavy-hearted. Everything
is God-like at this time of evening. Quietness
is the hush inside a cathedral.

Dogwoods pillar sky. I'm attending church
in my own backyard. Shrubs have dropped
another notch into darkness, become blackish
green. Blinking candles of fireflies light sacred
aisles of night. Dark reflects my silhouette
in the dining room window, superimposes it
on the sanctuary of my backyard as if I were
actually standing outside. The image doesn't last
long before complete darkness erases it.

A visit to a church, actual or imaginary, generates
serenity, temporary peace. I have not fallen
on my knees tonight for retribution of one
who has wronged me, nor have I have committed
heresy, so I will not be burned as Joan of Arc was, though
if I were to seek redemption, I would let fire purify me.

Through lights on Main Street, I see my reflection,
but I cannot see through my obfuscated heart
that is draped with night's black cloth.

## MILKWEED

Milkweed pods, shaped like oversized teardrops,
crack open. Tufts of angel hair swell outward
like white webs. On a gravel road, beside a field,
my camera shoots a close-up of an old
woman with hair white as pearls.
I touch the pod, its insides sticky with sap
and poison. I've read that monarch butterflies
feed on the bitter toxin, making them distasteful
to predators. I think about Friar Laurence's
speech in *Romeo and Juliet,* how the same
herb can be used for good or evil. Nearby,
a butterfly alights on a pod, not a monarch,
but yellow with black trim. I wouldn't pin it
to a board as some people do, but a telephoto
lens illuminates its antenna, thorax,
compound eyes, and proboscis. It flutters
to the next pod, hovers then lands. The wings
its only beauty, without them it's
an ugly insect. After a few more pictures,
I climb into my car, think about the
milkweed's bitter poison. American Indians
taught European settlers how to cook
the plant for safe consumption. Indians
also taught settlers to approach everything
for the good.

## TENDER BELIEVING

Splayed toward heaven, pummeled
against blustery rocks, the ocean models death.
Waves spiral upward, each in a cycle of seconds,
falls back into anonymity. I dally on the dock
for half an hour, study this watery repetition.
I'm shirtless. Sun feels like a cigarette burn
on my back. I watch gulls assault their prey,
extract it from current rolling to shore like empty,
wet coffins.

I rise from a sitting position, descend wooden steps
to the beach. Barefooted, I stand for a moment, tease
sand with my toes. It's almost two o'clock
in the afternoon, and I am getting too much sun.
I left my shirt in the coffee-colored cabin
along with my camera. I have been in the world
long enough not to be curious about sky. It's the sea
that I study, wonder if it is a forever entity,
something that will be there when graves are filled
with all of humanity.

Double-crested cormorants keep crossing my path,
as I continue down the beach, their feathers black
as a crow's. All the while, thunderous sound of the
Atlantic pounds in my ears. I think of Hart Crane
who must have thought there was nowhere else to go
but into turbulent depths. Jumping off the back
of a ship was his most memorable poem.

I clear my mind of reverie and start back. I will return
to the beach after dinner when the moon is a white stone,
an eye steering fishermen's boats, wrapping me in light
smooth as ermine, the creamy mantle I'll wear
under a ceiling of stars.

## SEVEN BUZZARDS IN MID-SUMMER

Seven buzzards landed on various antennae
of a cell phone tower a hundred feet from
my backyard. They sit still as statues
from Nichols Brothers Stoneworks. They
seem fixed in place for life, their stillness
a sad treachery to smaller birds. Occasionally,
one of them ascends, hovers, drifts back
to its perch two hundred feet in the air. I grab
binoculars, look at brown feathers, red tails
pointed downward, patient eyes focused on
possibility of carrion. Eventually, every antenna
is occupied like an open-air birdhouse. At times,
the buzzards' immobility imitates death.

I know next to nothing about buzzards, except
they dwarf most other birds. I have a secret ambition
to train a falcon, another predatory bird.
We would walk fields, discover rabbits and other prey.
The falcon would come back to my wrist
and alight there like a true friend,
a perennial companion. We would walk through all
seasons together, warm days of autumn,
unrelenting bite of winter, but always together.

It's been half an hour since I checked. When I do,
the antennae are vacant, the committee gone,
the kettle coasting on air currents to a different sky.

ROSES

Rose petals, dozens of red skiffs, drifted
to the ground, collected at the bottom
of stems like shipwrecked vessels.

After Mom's death, I attempted to revive
her rose garden, battled bugs, disease, but
one by one each bush died, in spite of
the work of bloodstained, thorn-bitten hands.
I breathe dismay when I think of the loss.
My scratched hands healed,
as insignificant suffering always does.

Fate stood at my back, watched me wheel
the hose in and out to no avail. Losing
Mom's roses crept into my dreams,
devoured peaceful sleep like weeping does.
What could I have done better to keep them
alive? Does it matter now?

Rabbits and squirrels cavort over wild grass
where American Beauty once thrived.
Whenever I walk past the overgrown garden,
voices like ghosts come from the ground.

Sun, the yellow face of death, hangs over
the small patch of earth I've abandoned.
Some days, I think of replacing the roses, but
I do not possess the touch, and I can be no more
than I can be.

## MORE THAN ROSES

Mom's rose garden bordered the back
of her house.  She coddled Golden Celebration,
Peace, American Beauty, Queen Elizabeth,
and  Mr. Lincoln.   All summer, her flowers
flamed flamboyant color.  She perfected
their care.  Now and then, she would snip one,
bring it inside.

The summer before she died, her roses darkened
with black spot.  Petals withered. No amount
of chemicals and care saved them. It was
as if they knew their keeper was darkening too.
Mom said not to worry because she planned
to dig them all up in the spring.

She died in February while thousands of
snowflakes, like shredded tissue,
collected on thorny canes.

Over time, I dug up the roses,
couldn't think of anything to replace them.

In winter, knee-deep snow
accumulated in the discarded bed.
From the window, I viewed mounds,
white as arctic bears, knew there was nothing beneath
but difficult memories.

## THE RISK OF ROSES

They validate brides, the dead, and Valentine's Day.
They are ladies of delicate disposition, demure
as a newlywed, perfumed as a Persian princess.

After several days of punishing sun,
their petals flatten, fade, and fall.
Spiny stems stand as sentries, protect
virtuous sweetness. A scald of thorns
scathes skin.

Roses are royalty among flowers.
Fancy names, fascinating colors predict
success in competitions.

They are most favored as shepherds
of love, communicating feelings
that connote deep connections.

The rose has, however, been known
to corrupt, to corrode in a vase
while its recipient recoils from burns
of disappointment and deception.

Then, a rose's petals become thin
as tissue paper, flutter down like
a pronouncement of infidelity.

# BEES WITHIN GOD'S SCHEME

A bee, flecked with pollen, as if caught
in a snow shower, curves into a hot blossom.
I watch pink sunrise pour over Rose of Sharon
and the backs of bees as they enter each flower.

I reach a hand into strangeness, see how close
fingers can play toward an insect before it pulls
loose from sticky pedals. To touch is the most
human gesture. To seek escape after intimate
nearness does not surprise. The bee rises
from beneath my hand, slips into a nearby flower,
sings a buzzing anthem.

Though this is a poem about touching
a bee with a promise not to hurt,
it's also about how mesmerizing their hunt is,
their entry into silky recesses to collect nectar.

They keep me company a bit longer,
loneliness somewhat lifting,
hunger our commonality.

I look up at scalloped clouds, porcelain cups
overflowing with honey-colored sun.

I rouse from a study of the bees,
content for a while to have been part of
their random religion.

## THE DIVING LESSON

I stood on the high dive all afternoon,
my feet concrete blocks, reluctant to bend
forward, to let gravity claim an eight-year-old.

Below me, water, blue as gas fire, lured,
but again and again I turned back toward the ladder.

At poolside, my camp counselor encouraged
confidence, his patience never waned.

Once more, I approached the end of the board,
brooding why I couldn't jump.  Fear
seemed too simple an explanation.

Finally, I figured it out.  Internal dialogue
had stopped me.  Only when I ceased thinking
did a blue chrysanthemum burst open
around my body, as if from the splash of a boulder,
and I bobbed to the surface, sun washing
across my smiling face.

## PALM POND

Frogs hide at the base of cattails,
bubble water when they lurch
from lily pads.  Sun burns the pond
into liquid aluminum.

I bend with camera to eye.
At this level, I'm looking through cattails
as if I had caged the sun. I move around
for different perspectives.

Two vacant benches sit at water's edge.
No one else is around until a woman
walking her dog appears at the opposite
end of the pond.  She passes me
without nodding or saying hello.

A quick click captures a crow.
It sails from a nearby tree,
circles the water, disappears like a speck
of soot. Sundown shadows lean
on sides of trees.  Last light tints
water pink.

I climb a knoll, frame a shot
before sun dissolves as if it were
a communion wafer.

In my car with windows down, I hear
crickets calibrate their legs.  Black streaks
of night-birds fly into trees.

I start the car.  Everything has become
invisible, value of my pictures very much
a substitute for a good friend.

## REMEMBERING AT PALM POND

Clouds accumulate, white as apple blossoms
edged with sun. It is a good picture-taking day.
I take a deep breath, point my camera, and shoot.
I'm standing on the shore of Palm Pond
beside cattails. Their flat, blade-like leaves
reach upward. A blue dragonfly hesitates
to land on my shoulder. I go from shot
to shot, lower the camera for a different
perspective. Sun is making me sleepy.
I'm becoming tired of the same scenery.

On the opposite bank, two preteen boys
and their dad lug fishing gear. Dad baits
the boys' hooks, helps them cast their lines.
I sneak a picture of the three, remembering
my dad's abusive fishing trips with me,
how unhelpful he was, drunk to the point
of sickness. It's not a scene I would take
a picture of, but it's an indelible presence
in my visual memory.

The boys and their dad settle into a still tableau,
Part of me wants to ignore their moment
of perfect harmony because I have learned
to live without it, but I can't stop staring.

A frog splashes out of the cattails.
Concentric circles open on the water.

I start home, lingering for one last look,
whispering "No" to my past.

# THE ARTIST OBSERVES A DEAD TREE

Five separate offshoots of one tree trunk twist
into each other.   It looks as if a giant has braided
the limbs together into one gnarled distortion.
Nothing is more naked than barren limbs
when everything understood about a tree is dead.
What illness killed the annual rings, or was it
stone-cold-nothing of old age that stripped it bare?
There will be no more listening to language
of restless leaves.  Maybe somewhere its heart
still struggles.  As one psychology book says,
everything has a psyche.

Someday, someone will paint, sculpt, or photograph it
because it is misshapened, malformed, and gnarled.
Some people hunger for the ugly, enjoy breathing
dark thoughts and even adore the deterioration of stars.

This tree is nothing now but a rupture in the earth
from which birds still speak echoes. This tree
represents impeccable death, wrapped in the question
of what it is still doing here?  Someday, an artist,
swayed by appreciation, sympathy, or regret, will paint
this tree that has poked a hole in heaven from which
a surprise of butterflies will pour out of the opening.

# SEAGULLS AT McGREGOR BAY, CANADA

Cousin Dute stabs a perch to a board
with a pick. I stand close by, hear the pluck
of the point pierce the wood.
He severs its head, slices the body open,
separates it, cleans out intestines.

Seagulls, looking for loose morsels,
sail out of pines that edge the bay,
shoot from clouds like feathered bullets.
Their menacing shrieks echo overhead
before they land, close wings, sit waiting
for leftovers. I watch, mesmerized
by their determination.

Dute never tries to divert the birds.
He lets them swoop for leftovers, circle
the dock to dine on death's detritus.

The gulls scavenge much of the afternoon,
closing beaks around entrails entangled
in blood. As my aunt Liz used to say,
"Everything has to eat. Everything wants
to live."

That night, we fry thick, golden fillets
served with corn on the cob. From inside
the house, I can still hear gulls squawking
like hopeful children who won't take no
for an answer.

## HUMMINGBIRD WITH FOLDED WINGS

One evening, while watering hydrangea,
a hummingbird landed on a yew
a foot from me. Aside from the fact that
it was so close, I'd never seen a hummingbird
fold its wings. It trusted me enough to rest
within my reach. I took it as an omen
of good luck.

I'd like to believe the bird alighted just for me
which would throw the whole occurrence
into a philosophical realm. Was it just for me,
or was it purely chance fooling me
with a bit of holiness?

Even the water fountaining from the hose
didn't frighten it, but when I moved
from a sideways glance into a full view,
the bird had disappeared.

I can't complain. A glimpse
of its rainbow feathers was enough.
I can only speak about how chosen I felt.

Probably such an experience
will never happen to me again. I felt
as if I were having a moment in church when
the very structure itself, high ceilings, stained
glass silence, makes belief possible. Those
sacred seconds saved an otherwise derailed day.

# THE THICKET

The front of my tee-shirt stuck to my chest.
It was a brown July, extra hot.
I'm talking about high-90s everyday.
What they used to call an old-fashioned summer.
It seemed as if it took extra years for me
to reach ten years old. Maybe things just grew
slower in the 1940s.

Angie, my age, also lived on Barthman Avenue.
We often sang popular songs together,
played cowboys. She insisted on being
sheriff, while I was relegated to robbing banks.

On this particular day, people stayed inside
because it was too hot to be out. She, however,
wanted to walk several miles down South High
Street to a small wooded area which seemed
an unusual place for a dense stand of trees
with constant traffic streaming by.

She tugged at my resistance until I relented,
and we began to trudge the several miles.
I think she had a crush on me. Sometimes,
she would act funny, lean into me, then
back off as if it were an accidental closeness.

We reached the pathless woods, parted
tree branches, and entered. I couldn't have
felt hotter if I had been dropped into a toaster slot.

It was dense, dark, and buggy.   Mosquitoes
stuck to our sweaty faces. That's when
we exited to the street, started back home,
satisfied to have made the journey.

It wasn't until years later I realized
how much that ten-year-old girl loved me,
and how close I came that day to being kissed.

# FRANKLIN CONSERVATORY

All walks lead through leafy greenery.
Splashes of sun dapple Chinese Banyan
and Golden Gate Fig. Trunks of Ficus
twisted around each other, like arms forced
out of their natural shape, form a
conglomerate of woody stems. Palm branches
and coleus frame exotic plant collections
and lush floral displays. In the Pacific
Island Water Garden, a rainbow of
butterflies fly freely. They seek open
flowers, hover, fold and unfold wings,
flit to the next flower. A waterfall roars
down a rocky slope, gushes into a stony
spillway. I look upward at Chihuly ceilings,
see all colors of the spectrum blown
into glass flower shapes, overlapping and
transparent. On a table, incandescent
light through cubes, bowls, and spheres
is a life-size kaleidoscope, a
polychromatic gift for the eyes.
At the exit, I touch glossy leaves,
marvel at large pots of Desert Plains
fountain grass and gigantic plum-colored
fronds. Reluctantly, I drive away from Eden.

## STORM BOUND

I'm on the front porch in a rocker,
pumping my feet. Clouds black as giant
bears hang overhead. Thunder makes
the sky sound angry as it blurts out
lightning. Mom's voice behind me
says come into the house away from
danger. My deeper impulse defies her,
and I stay in the rocker. The strobes
of lightening continue to create seconds
of amplified daylight. Like a fist
beating on a sheet of metal, thunder
reverberates, and the sky pounds
the ground with a downpour. I linger
on the porch as if tied to the storm
by an umbilical cord that feeds me
its fury. When it stops, a nascent glow
highlights leaves, and a red and yellow
sunset tints whole trees. Birds step out
on branches, and the moon, at the opposite
end of the sky, slowly rises like something
prehistoric shining its white bones.

# THE TEACHER OF STORMS

Mom and I huddle on the patio swing,
watch sky darken to gray. Thunder grumbles
a staccato of drum beats. Sprinkles of rain,
the size of ants, blow toward us. The storm
approaches from southwest. A canopy
of rolling clouds slides over our heads.
We scoot to the edge of our seats, anticipate
the inevitable. A harpoon of lightning arcs
in the distance, splits sky in half. That's when
all ninety-four years of mom reaches
for her cane. She stands, and I help her
into the house.

She closes kitchen curtains, plops into a rocker,
proselytizes about safety measures to take.

As a kid, her mother made her
and her sisters and brothers pray during a storm.
When I was a kid, Mom ushered me into a closet
where we sat quiet until the disturbance passed.
During those times, I felt as if I were in a stalled
elevator.

When I grew up, contrary to her teaching,
I loved storms. I've snapped many photos
of threatening skies and serrated teeth
of lightning as its electricity whitened the earth.

## BEACH, PATH, SEA

On Sanibel Island, I walk alone
along the sea, leave behind a dead self
like a piece of driftwood with my name
on it.

Separate for a while from my brother
and his wife, otherwise good company,
I value time by myself with woods
on one side and water on the other.

The plan is to discover a new reverence.
The walk over sand is poetry beneath
a benediction of sun.  With voracious
hunger, cormorants dive from cloud cliffs.
I amble beyond the predictable, eliminate
inner commentary, simply watch and listen
to the swoop of squeaking seagulls
snapping up what swims beneath them.

This is my time to become removed
for a while, abandoned to nothing more
than shelling.  I am good at that with
an accurate eye for conch and junonia.

I turn around, start back toward
the rented house, big as a mansion, where
I will sit down and read a book,
remember everything I noticed
each unspoken second beside the sea.

## SHELL HUNTING

Like transparent silk, ocean unfolds
at my feet. Foam lingers around ankles.
I comb along the beach searching
for a Junonia shell. The beach is rich
with Conch Shells, but no Junonia.

I spot a Sand Dollar, rinse it off.
Its five leaf-like petals form
a kind of star at the center.

I wade in the baptismal implication
of surf, continue to hunt for a Junonia,
settle for tulip-banded shells
and the hint of religion strolling the shore
of an ocean affords.

When I return to the rented house,
I wash sand from the shells, polish them.
A small, pink sunset tinged with yellow
and orange shines inside the Conch.

I handle the sand dollar with care.
It is the delicate wafer on the tongue
of the ocean like the Holy communion
that resides somewhere inside of me,
somewhere.

## LOOKING FOR SHELLS ON SANIBEL ISLAND

I scoop up a conch shell, one of several.
I want a lightning whelk, but
tide does not bring them ashore here.

I fill my pockets with shells, pour out sand,
rinse them in surf. They are veils of death
creatures have crept into the world from.
I am hesitant to wade into deeper
water where the helpless have wailed
from the slice of a random shark.

Sun is hot as inside a clenched fist.
Gulls rake claws over shallows, drag up
flinching fish. I've walked about a mile
among egrets, ospreys, American white ibises.

When I start back, the dazzling knife of sun
has dulled to shadows of sundown.
Mansions to my right seem empty,
nobody turning eyes toward passersby.

Pink trims horizon. Shifting, melancholy light
moves me to want a human companion, someone
heading home like myself who will be with me
when geese fly high and evening becomes a hint
of blue.

# ONE OF THE HOTTEST SUMMERS ON RECORD

Sun breaks open, releases bayonets
of heat, drives dozens of birds to the birdbath.
I tie tomato plants to blazing steaks, drain
boiling water from the hose. Week after week,
thermostats register over ninety degrees.

Bees melt into cup-like flowers of
rose of Sharon. To stir a little breeze,
I swing on the back porch, think about
my stepdad in the local cemetery,
beneath a tombstone. I visualize
a cross section of ground, the vault
pressed down by weight of eternity,
latch of death locking him into
perpetual stasis.

I'm drenched in sweat. Suffocated sky
has closed down on the earth like the lid
of a waffle iron. I asked myself if
appreciation of being alive is a sin
against the dead? I can't answer.
I can only continue to swing
and wait for a breeze.

## A SHADOWY TALE OF SUMMER

Two preteen boys drowned fishing off the damn
one summer day. I always remember
that accident when driving on Greenlawn
Avenue along the Scioto River.

Plenty of people fish there. These boys
were by themselves, perhaps hoping
for a catch that would be much talked about.

I picture them wearing baseball caps,
taking an occasional look up, squinting
into intense sun. They lay bait can and
stringer on shore, took small steps
into shallow water that slipped over the dam
like liquid silk, frothed and foamed
as if full of detergent when it hit the river.

One boy's line snagged on a drifted log.
It must have frightened him to wade into
fringe of surf below the dam, but he did.
Undercurrent sucked him beneath the surface.
He grabbed at water. The other boy attempted
rescue, followed the first into riptide.

A passerby saw the struggle.
By the time he notified authorities, both
boys had disappeared. Fishing lines leaped,
tossed in the current, frantic, convulsive jerks
alive above the dead
they later dragged the bottom for.

## ODE TO OHIO CORNFIELDS

For miles, monotony of cornfields, green
as gooseberry, stream by car windows.
Tassels blow in the wind like beachcombers'
yellow hair. Leaves, lofty scepters, rule
stocks deep into August soil, hide cobs
that sweeten by the hour. Soon enough,
moonlight will turn these stocks into eerie,
neck-tall phantoms.

Halfway to my destination, I'm still among
farm-size fields over which hawks and crows
screech garbled grammar. Row after row
of uniformity hypnotizes. Like a cyan cyclorama,
blaze of blue sky curves down behind the corn.

In a few weeks, combines will reap, thresh,
winnow, leave behind stubble of death.
I imagine the inevitable future of these crops,
most harvested to shanks and husks,
others attached to posts like pagan sacrifice
or made into decorative displays of demise
at roadside markets.

# AUTUMN

*Whoever has no house now, will*
*never have one.*
*Whoever is alone will stay alone,*
*will sit, read, write long letters*
*through the evening,*
*and wonder along boulevards,*
*up and down,*
*restlessly, while dry leaves are*
*blowing.*

--Reiner Maria Rilke

*Autumn shows us*
*how beautiful it is*
*to let things go*

--Unknown

## WHERE AUTUMN COMES FROM

The door swings open on decay,
and summer slips away like a silk scarf
in a breeze.  Scarlet and yellow leaves
stumble from windy branches.  Blue sky
bends around blighted sycamores.  Black
as sunflower seeds, crows shriek in a barrage
of staccato notes.  Autumn saturates
the air with the scent of burning pine logs,
and bulges the coffers of sycamores
with gold coins.  During this blustery day,
bees burden their wings with cream-colored
dust from the Rose of Sharon, and gardens
continue to wither in the glare of late sun.

I wonder around the yard learning
over and over from the trees how
each year orange tints and magenta hues
come back like an annual promise.
They scribble a signature of loss,
teach me how death can be
the origin of perfect beauty.

# WHAT TO SAY AND FEEL IN AUTUMN

Maple leaves, red quilt pieces, lie beneath
the tree.  A light breeze sews them together.
If it could talk, the tree would be indifferent
to loss.

I forget language, look past words at an
inexpressible day of sky blue as Crater Lake.
A rage of sun, banana-skin yellow, sculpts
landscape in dazzling light. These are
my thoughts as I let go of the last hours
of summer and prepare for first frost.

I count down days in the last week
of September, remember driving
to southern Ohio on blue days like
today, cruising by farm fields full
of apricot-colored pumpkins.

At this moment, I'm in my backyard
with a peck basket, gathering apples
groundhogs haven't eaten. It is a sad tree
that has become skeletal. Soon, I will
call a tree service and have it cut down.
The smell of its innermost wood will
permeate the air, and I will breathe in
nostalgia, picture the day Mom planted it
twenty years ago. For now, I watch
its leaves collect on the ground, unhappiness
of death crackling under my feet like cellophane.

## THE INEXPRESSIBLE RAPTURE OF AN
## AUTUMN DAY

Late September rain sobs on the windshield.
Wipers sweep away walls of water.
Leaf colors are faint and indistinct.
A sudden ribbon of sunlight streams from gray
clouds along sky's edges. The unexpected shaft
of golden light fans down to earth, and rain stops.

The whole sun creeps out, brightens yellow
sugar maples, red sourwood. I stop the car,
ogle intense tints and hues.

My grandma Mohr came from these hills.
She and my grandpa married on Potts Hill
in the Schmidt's, of sausage fame, house
a few miles from Bainbridge, Ohio.
I remember bringing Mom here.
She pointed to the window of the second-story
bedroom where her parents stayed.
Death has danced away my family, but
I'm lucky Mom showed me the past.

I start the car, turn onto a gravel road
where mascaraed leaves curl like magenta
and purple eyelashes, begin to blink
twilight shadows.

I drive back to the highway, think
sometimes an aimless journey is
the perfect trip.

## OCTOBER FEELS LIKE A PLACE

It's where yellow leaves unfasten from birch
trees, and the smell of woodsmoke prevails.
It's a place near a pumpkin patch where
you turn the last page before winter.
It's crows on a cornfield fence rail, black
throats rattling caws.  It's a place where
a profusion of chrysanthemums suddenly
mean more than any other flower.
It's where walking in leaves is absolute
contentment, where coming upon a hillside
of crayoned trees or leaving footprints
in early morning frost are surprise gifts.
It is a place where an enormous white moon
quickens the pulse, a place where nostalgia
gushes up from contemplation and throws
longing into gear.  Mark October a place
where a multitude of bones, bats, and black
cats fill imagination with a flutter of welcome
fear, and you recoil from the rat-a-tat-tat
of a witch's fingernails on your window.
It's where roadside markets display a dozen
different baskets of apples, and jugs of cider,
the color of sunset, become broth of the season.
Let someone special stand in this place with you.
Let leaves fall around you both and feel
nothing less than love.

## OCTOBER'S CONTRADICTORY PROMISE

Today speaks a language
with no grammatical rules.
A sentence of sycamore
slips its yellow adjectives
to the ground in continuous
succession.

I speak inward,
articulate names of other trees.
maple and elm loosen
leaves upward
in a breeze-bound bouquet.

Monotonous sky, blue
as a lily pond, curves
downward, edges
a ruby and rust
chrysanthemum garden.

This is
how life can end
with lush insistence
of heightened color,
counterfeit promises
and the illusion
of new beginnings
before limbs become bare,
and the lie becomes laden
with thousands of snowflakes
and the heartbreak of winter

## RAIN RITUAL

An endless day of October drizzle
drains from the dogwood tree, pools
beneath it with bottomless reflections.
Everywhere inside, light is gray
as stone, and spirits of family members
haunt me:

My stepdad slumps in his recliner.
Baseball register spread over his lap,
he records statistics, pencil diligent
as a scribner's. One small lamp,
like a personal secret, illuminates
his scratchpad.

Mom throws an occasional glance
out the kitchen window, as if a scowl
could change weather. She washes
potatoes in the porcelain sink,
peels each in one continuous move.
Skins hang in mid-air like brown snakes.

They say nothing, but I can see them
breathe before shadows of what killed
them enter the room, stop imagination.

Rain skims windows now.
I feel chilled, loss that makes
each day's journey infinite.

I have to release them.  I have to accept
death has a place in this house
as much as recollection.

## THE HALLOWEEN PARTY

For a month, Mom and her sister, Mary,
planned a Halloween party for friends
in their eighth-grade class. They pocketed
their ten cents per day for lunch.

By the week of Halloween, they had saved
enough for crepe paper and jelly beans.
All through the girls' planning, their dad
remained silent, the epitome of nonchalance,
a weasel in a hole waiting to snap a chicken's
neck. His ears were shut to their talk.

In class, Freddie Schmidt, whose dad owned
Schmidt's Sausage, sat behind Mom, promised
to donate wieners and buns.

The day before the party, sisters strung crepe
paper streamers, filled dishes with jelly beans.

Halloween night, their dad lounged
in his recliner beneath orange and black
streamers. When he heard a knock at the door,
he barked, "I'll get it." He put his newspaper down,
ripped the door open. Freddy's arms balanced
boxes. Their dad huffed, "What do you want?"
A turtle retracting its head, Freddy answered,
"I've come to Dorothy's party." With his hand
on the doorknob their dad blurted, "There's no party
here."

Next day at school, Freddie and classmates
sung a constant chorus of ridicule.
"How did you like Mary and Dorothy's party?
Wasn't it swell?" For days, embarrassment
followed the girls around like a rabid dog
while their father never spoke a word either way.

## A HALLOWEEN POEM

The three-story, pre-Civil-War house creaks.
It's gray, unfinished clapboard sags.
Spider webs wreath its windows. In each,
a jack-o'-lantern flickers bright yellow.
Tombstones in the mouth of the neighboring
churchyard are moonlit teeth crooked as
arthritic hands. A picket fence encompasses
the house.  Its jagged spears impale low
cumulus clouds that roll from a black sky.
Wind whips walls of leaves against
trick-or-treaters.

A man's silhouette, a bent branch, creeps
from street to bush, lunges from house
to house, staying only for seconds
in side yards.  His bony, long fingers bear
a scythe. His ebony cape rides wind.
He is not in costume.
He is real as the everlasting.

When he approaches the three-story house,
his knock echoes to the cupola.
The door, no one wants to answer, squeaks open.
Only swirls of air greet him. He curses
at those who evade, who last longer
than he expected.  He turns away.
The door slams shut, and he banishes
like sleep in the morning.
The jack-o'-lanterns sneer.

RENICK'S FARM

I'm standing near a rail fence, looking
at a field of pumpkins, orange as goldfish,
round as moons, as many as stars in the sky.
Paths lead between rows, but I'm satisfied,
as an otter in mud, to meander on this side
of the fence.

I don't carve them anymore since my family
died.  If I did, I'd make a pumpkin with sad eyes,
downturned mouth.  Celebrating Halloween
seems far away from my desire
to unfold paper decorations, purchase candy
corn.  If I dressed, I'd go as a pauper of love.

I look around the farm, want to buy apples,
taste sweet juice that's been building beneath
the skin since summer.  I pay for a pound
of Gala, glance at the car, deposit the fruit
in the trunk.

At the car, I see the sun's shadows start
to cross the gravel drive, but sky is still
blue as a lazuli bunting or unfulfilled wishes.
I'm near a pyramid of pumpkins, corn
shocks tied to roof posts, straw bales.

People pass me in pairs, pushing carts
full of fresh peaches, sweet potato pies,
goat milk fudge, Indian corn.

How did it happen that I got so far away
from commemorating Halloween, from
wanting the touch of another person's hand?

## THE FULL WORTH OF AN AUTUMN
## AFTERNOON

Maple leaves, red as hot coals, curl, break off,
litter lawn like death tokens. Sun infuses
cooler air with just enough warmth to warrant
a sweater. The smell of burning leaves
drifts from a neighbor's yard next door.

I grab a rake from the garage, began pulling
leaves into a pile. The sky is clear, blue
as a bachelor button. An uplifting emotion
pervades the day, and I am filled with light.
I've boarded a day in October as I would a bus
taking me among chrysanthemums, sweet
Autumn clematis, purple coneflowers,
touch-me-nots.

Again and again, I drag the rake towards me,
fit into this day as if it were a temperate shirt
just my size. I feel the truth of being,
truth that doesn't have a definition beyond
satisfaction from flowers, sun, and sky.

I fight the impulse to want someone beside me
who appreciates a perfect day, but that would
only complicate the moment. In the end,
it is enough to be a recipient, to stand very still
with rake in hand, remind myself I want nothing
more than to be overwhelmed with being alive.

## DISTANT BONFIRE

Tonight I'm not far from Columbus where
landscape becomes pastoral, and acres of corn
stubble tell the story of an earlier crop.

I park on the side of a rural road, step outside.
The moon, carved with the face of a man
 over forty, hangs like a white pumpkin in the sky.

A rail fence outlines a field that swallows
moonlight.  Hundreds of feet across the field,
a farmhouse fits snug in the night.  Orange
flames from a bonfire, night's lantern,
flare upward, throw elongated shadows
against the house.

Several people linger near the fire, faces
distorted like Halloween masks. Someone stirs
burning logs.  Flames and sparks soar
upward, dazzle the dark.

I'm tempted to cross the field, join the group.
On such a cold, October night,
they would welcome a stranger
who has stumbled upon their hospitality,
but maybe not.

I climb back into my car, leave the bonfire
for someone else to find, feeling fortunate
to have had even a glimpse of its beneficent light.

## THE LEAF

Like a withered hand, the golden leaf hangs
on the limb, a brittle angel with one wing.
I like that it hasn't fallen yet, and wonder
where its heart is. My eyes fill with its
imminent deterioration, waiting for it
to fall, but it doesn't. The sun's fire makes
me blink. Maybe the leaf will burn. Most
likely a breeze will lift it into a spin
to the ground. Rain will tarnish its stunning
color, hold it in place until a day rolls it up
like a cigar, or it gets raked into a dark bag
where even the bravest don't want to go.
I can't, in the meantime, stop the dying.
If I were to snap it off and press it
in a book, it would become a ghost
of itself, faded, fragile as old skin.
Every death brings me closer to life.

## DAYS OF FEVER

I'm bedridden with rheumatic fever,
have been for three months.  I know
it's autumn because sun has shifted
to the south, throws a blanket of light,
the color of gold bullion, all afternoon
across my bed.  Moreover, maple leaves,
red as fever, dance past my window.
I spend many hours making finger rings
from tiny beads, string them in a tight circle,
sell them to relatives who come to visit.

Dr. Guthrie, our family doctor, has twice
dragged his new piece of medical equipment
up twenty steps to our apartment on Barthman
Avenue.  He uses his new machine to take
an electrocardiogram of my seven-year-old heart.
He calls it an EKG.  He is a young doctor who,
just starting out, has hope that I will recover.

A knock at the front door awakens me
from an early-evening doze.  Aunt Ada
and Uncle Heinie bring a touch of elegance
to the foot of my bed.  She wears a black hat
with a small feather.  A fox-fur coat makes
her look 1940's stylish.  Uncle Heinie sports
a wool felt fedora and a gray topcoat to match.
They've brought me the only thing I have
so far requested.  Aunt Ada holds a miniature
cash register, a toy I saw in a catalog.
I take it from her with much gratitude.

Before they leave, she kisses my forehead.
He does the same. I am used to his affection.
He is of French descent.

After they leave, I fall asleep visualizing
the time when I will be well enough
to step out again onto the front porch.

## LEAVES

Death of leaves woos me.

I saw a couple dancing beneath yellow
maple. As they danced, leaves spiraled
about their feet.

A husband, whose wife succumbed
to pneumonia, took her among leaves
in a cemetery and buried her.

Icarus fell into leaves the color of sun.

I know these things are true. This poem is
made of leaves, red, orange, faint blue
in the shadows.

Like leaves, I have begun to let go.

I imagine myself in midair, body straight out,
parallel to solitude, skimming gentle fear
of spin and drift, the dizzying twirl
that brings sheen of sweat to my face.

And then I take the leaves into myself
because initiation into October
has always been done this way.

## RAKING

Dead leaves grow red, detach, waddle down.
Ground is thick with autumn's signature.
It seems I'm raking the same leaves
from the same spot that I did last year.
Past few days have been quiet
as a cathedral, so what renegade breeze
brought them down? Was it the sudden swoosh
of wind that slipped by me as I slept?
Bare brown limbs snag on silky sky blue
as bellflowers. If the tree were a post office,
and each leaf a letter, autumn's mail
would have been delivered on time.
Sun melts over my back like soothing hands
that never move away.

My neighbor burns a leaf pile.
Acrid sweetness of smoke drifts into my yard
like a woodland perfume.

It's a glorious day, everything tinted
the color of a tawny haystack, not quite yellow,
but blond with a slight tarnish. I am wearing
a motley-colored, CPO jacket and remorse
about misplaced love. If I rake long enough,
maybe I can get to the other side of self-reproach,
About now, I have my own leaf pile to burn
along with regret for having fallen prey
to a predatory user.

I strike a match. Smokey fire rolls upward.
I stand back from flames, want nothing more
than forgetting the impossibility of forgetting.

## RANDOM REFLECTIONS WHILE RAKING
## AUTUMN LEAVES

The pungent sweetness of smoke rises
from a leaf pile.  When I'm finished raking,
I'll carve pumpkin faces for front steps,
tie corn shocks around porch posts,
prepare for beggars approaching my house
for candy.

I'm almost finished, stuffed forty bags
with maple and sycamore leaves.
I stand still, think how can there be more?

Along with leaves, so many other things fall
away: days, lives, chances. Someday, I will be
autumn.  Foliage of my life become irretrievable
yesterdays.  My trunk will become crooked,
gnarled, my face, wrinkled and worn.

I drag each bag to the side of the garage
until Waste Management picks up on Thursday.

It is dark when I finish. Timers have turned on
candles in the window., a sign of welcome
from colonial times. When I enter the garage
to hang the rake on a hook, I notice another rake
with several of last year's leaves pierced by tines.
I want to hear the leaves talk about what they know
and remember.  Do they recall my failures,
aspirations.  My left hand reaches;
I crumble the leaves, drop them into a waste basket.

In the house, I sit in a chair by the living room window, stare at a candle, a beacon to someone far far in the distance.

## HOW MANY MORE YEARS WILL I BE
## RAKING LEAVES


A fist of wind upsweeps oak leaves, maroon
as beets. Most of the day, I've been standing
in leaves, raking, wishing I had a wand
that would bunch them up, but
they keep coming down, fluttering
on and on like one of Mahler's symphonies.

I used to look forward to autumn,
swirling blades and petioles of a closing season.
This afternoon, however, I work slower.

On Monday, my doctor will ask if
I've been short of breath. I'll tell him
I wanted the leaves to have wings and fly away
on their own. He will laugh, write a prescription.

I stand still holding the rake like a staff.
My hand is ready to bleed from a blister.
I am streaked with sweat and lost in fatigue.
Like many birthdays forgotten, I can't remember
the first time I ever did this raking routine.
The answer is to work in small spaces, not
feel desolate when breezes become the enemy.

Finished bagging, I drag the rake to the garage,
dream of spring and of being surrounded by flowers.

# AN AUTUMN ROOM

It seems as if the dogwood tree has turned
maroon within minutes. Behind it, sun bulges
with light. A flawless sky blazes
cornflower blue. Birds follow secret routes
along the curve of the earth. As I look out
the dining room window, I see a perfect
autumn day in my backyard. Sun, a white,
hot pearl, only as big as a button, warms me
through glass, wheels over my body,
becomes hot as a match. I lean away from
the window, seek a cooler place in the room.

I move a little into shadows away from sun
and the likelihood of love. I have
learned to stand aside and not let myself
be exposed to possibility. Soon, I will
make room in my day for writing,
tell about how I am a hundred victims
of my own heart.

## AN ABBREVIATED AUTUMN DAY

Crimson oak leaves shiver loose; yellow sycamore
drift down like golden suns. It's no secret autumn
inspires longing, quickens the pulse to want something
indefinable. As day goes on, in counterpoint to twilight,
tree shadows lengthen across the lawn like ebony hints
of where they fell from. During last hours of daylight,
birds in birdbath still bathe in blue reflections
of the sky and in remaining cloud wisps thin
as violin string, white as whipped cream.

Melancholy assails the mind with sweet sadness,
seeps under the skin, infuses every part of the body
with appreciation for trees rainbowized by death.

Squirrels understand the world better than people.
Each day they negotiate winter by tucking acorns
into pockets of earth. There will be no poverty in
squirrel-land.

Night Comes. The moon slips upward  Somehow,
birds and squirrels vanish before anyone can
figure out they've disappeared. Black as a panther,
night paws its way across landscape.  Someone
on a porch watches a star leave the heavens,
maybe makes a wish not realizing it's pointless.

## POTTS HILL

Light flickers through windshield.
It's an ideal autumn day, sun sharp as a nail.
I drive into the country to see fading leaves,
their extravagant tints, hues. Turning
onto a gravel road that winds around Potts Hill,
I steer beneath a waterfall of yellow oak,
stare at flaxen fields that border forests
of blazing red and orange.

I pull to the side of the road, stumble out
to snap a photo. Locusts lull me
with their monotonous lullaby. I lean
against the rail fence. Clouds open
wings, fly overhead in sky, blue
as the center of a gas flame. A murder
of crows explodes from the
ruptured air with discordant caws.
A hint of sundown shadows leaves.

This is the kind of moment when
I remember the dead because I am alive
to see vibrant foliage, to breathe in
the scent of woodsmoke.

I return to the car, weight of ponderous
dusk at my back disconnecting me
from a day perfect as the body in sleep.

# A POEM WITH MANY R'S

Oak leaves redden, relinquish their hold
on black limbs. I rethink the season,
realize dying reawakens beauty. The release
of leaves randomizes my thoughts, and
I recall my mother's last moments.

At the end, she received life support,
the regularized hiss of finishing life
at the end of a tube. I realize someone
would see falling away from pain as
redemption. I renounce the tendency
to romanticize decay. Rouged leaves
teach deception, but I've never seen
a tree reclaim its foliage as a remedy
for loss. It's called resurrection.
I suppose that's the soul's way
of reviving mortality . The ultimate
rewinding. I resist retreating into
religion, its assurance that decay is
temporary, the rolling away of the stone
guaranteed. I rip up such doctrine
that relies on conjecture.

Autumn leaves rot on the ground.
There is no retreat from their finality
or the truth of why they turn red.
They rubricate the manuscript of death
with a capital "D."

# THE WATERS OF AUTUMN

Maple Leaves
are golden harbors
on which
ships of sun bob
in and out,
in and out,
of light and shadow.

Wind lifts
ship's harbors.
They oscillate
downward.

I stand in
yellow,
yield to crackle
of finality underfoot,
the sound
of lost friendship,
melancholy
of resignation,
of almost drowning
during a season
away from shore.

# A NOVEMBER LIFE

Diane has taken up knitting.
She sags in an occasional chair
by the casement window. The mantel
clock tick-tocks language of lost hours.
Late afternoon sun makes transparent art
on hardwood floor.

She's seventy-two, doesn't know how
to dismiss the thought she has nothing
to expect but death.

She reads Shakespeare, listens to Mahler,
makes ceramic Christmas trees. Once,
she had a romantic relationship with a man
named Paul. They had worked together
in the state office building downtown where
she handled clerical tasks. He was her supervisor.
She wasn't prepared for love to tire so soon.

"Men," she thinks, "are never as present
as they appear to be, roving among detritus
of their own egos."

Autumn light becoming less, she places
her knitting on a side table, wraps a coat around her
shoulders.  Outside, on the back patio, she breaks bread
for birds, stands still, watches sunset dissolve.

After sun has cooled, she ambles back inside,
snaps on a lamp that throws a circle of light
on the table.  Unfinished knitting lies within the glow.

## A NOTE ON NOVEMBER

The day, gray as smoke, starts out rainy.
Trees retain a modicum of color. Muted
rust, faded-green forest skirt the highway.
Chalky-white sky hangs like a funeral
shroud over ruins of autumn. A dozen
times a day, geese fly over Heron Pond.
Raindrops, transparent pebbles, smear
on the window, slide down the glass
over and over.

Leaves are lost for good.
There is an emptiness about the trees.
From a radio on my desk, I hear a forecast
of incipient snow. People will remove
their heavier coats from plastic bags, bargain
with fate for better weather.

Meanwhile, the old stand in the wings,
trudge around in a late autumn room,
talk of long-ago harvests and hand-picked
apples, wait for an unexpected pinch of sun.

The young talk of love and glamour, dream
of lying down together in goldenrod and flax,
oblivious of the sound of dead leaves
scraping along sidewalks.

## EVALUATING THE PROVINCE OF NOVEMBER

Heavy rain, slashing against the window,
turns afternoon into gloom. This
glad-to-be-inside kind of day can only be
brightened by lamplight.

Outside the window, capricious branches
of oak, black as an undertaker's clothes,
thrash against one another.  Left-over leaves,
hang in the dogwood, remnants of torn rag.

I slip into a coat, take a walk just to feel
the difference when I return to the door that
opens from this day's threatening winds
to warmth from a stack of logs on the grate.

# A THANKSGIVING VARIATION

Looking out a window, I understand
how dying works. An uncommon blaze
of blue sky catches in bare branches
of the ravaged oak. I watch red leaves
break free, follow one another
in sinuous paths downward.
Turning away, I settle into a chair
near the fireplace.

The introspective mood, induced by
firelight, reminds me of relatives
who will not come to dinner this holiday,
or ever again. This thought fills my heart
with cold.

After several temperate days,
The Weather Channel forecasts snow
accompanied by withering winds.
One storm window, minus a screw, bangs.
in the breeze. Streets seem empty,
this house vacant.

I've chosen to skip celebration and dinner
conversation comprised of constant references
to spouses, children, and grandchildren.
An outcast from those sacred realms,
I would slouch in a chair, feel defeated.
Instead, I'm prepared to stay home, keep company
with the ticking of the clock, put sticks on the fire,
echo my own thoughts into memory.

## THANKSGIVING PRELUDE

It is one week before Thanksgiving.
I'll eat dinner in the afternoon
at my brother's. Memories will haunt.
I will feel greedy to want my parents,
aunts, uncles back. Since they have all
died, I have not found a successful
something to replace them.

At home, when twilight is an hour away,
I will take a walk, listen to leaves
crackle underfoot, light a fire and hear it
crackle too. As if they had breath to hold,
dogwood tree, burning bushes, tree
on the property line will appear ready
to bear the hurt of winter.
Their stillness of branches is equal to stillness
in an empty church.

Dark will come, and I will enter the house.
Silence will follow me in like an invisible
hound. My world will become small
as the beak of a snowbird pecking for seed
along the backyard sidewalk until the bird disappears
into what seems a trick of the lonely dark.

I will strike a match to kindling in the fireplace,
bronze glow of flame rush to my face.
Logs will hiss, sparks loosen and fly upward
away from the room in which I have become
a shadow.

## GO NICELY

Our house on Moler Road is buried
underground, sold to a real estate
developer, demolished by a demolition
crew. A waterbed and upright Steinway
piano were left behind, plowed under.
Hard-hatted men bulldozed the house
into piles of debris they hauled away
in dump trucks.

I watched this destruction
from the next door neighbor's yard.
The image of one remaining wall and
a closet with my brother's rain coat
dangling from a hanger seemed fit
for a Fellini movie or an epitaph
for all my parents had ever worked for.
The property became a paved parking lot
for semis.

I have never returned to a neighborhood
that drove my parents away because of crime,
not even for nostalgia's sake. They would
have liked to remain on Moler until death,
but the house died first.

Thanksgiving comes to memory
as an example of holidays celebrations
on Moler Road. Aunt Liz, Aunt Ada,
and Mom attempting to stay out

of each other's way in the kitchen
and yet compatible, is one of many
recollections that did not get bulldozed.

My family moved to a small town. Their
house, on a dead-end road, resembled
their old house. They were happy to be away
from living behind locked doors, barred windows.
That first year, they began a new Thanksgiving,
were beautifully satisfied with the change.

## NOTES ON AN ICE-COVERED DAY

Half the light of day is gone, and fires
of the sun have disappeared under a cloud
cover. Like glass bicycle spokes,
rain-frozen limbs gouge air and gloom.
The day looks like the first hour of the earth
before haze lifted,

I stand at the window with hands stuffed
into deep warmth of pockets. It's three o'clock
in the afternoon, and I can't shake chill
permeating walls. When I turn from
the window, rooms are dark enough
to warrant lamplight.

Tonight I am moderator at the Al-Anon meeting.
I have chosen the topic of anger for discussion.
I often wrestle with a tendency to anger. I have
slammed doors, bellowed curses, pitched sarcasm
faster than a ninety-mile-an-hour baseball.
Gradually, I have learned to cup hand over mouth
when my tongue is aflame with fury.

I scribble final notes at the desk, switch off
the light, return to the window. I have not seen
a squirrel or a bird all day. It's as if nature's magic
made them disappear .

Although it is only mid-November, I wait for spring,
breathe air into my hands, to thaw these icy days.

## NEGOTIATING THE LAST DAY OF NOVEMBER

Early dusk bespeaks the clock's new hours.
A heavy wind combined with gloom foretells
a storm is on the way. It could be rain slicing
at windows or whirlwinds of snow.

Dogwood branches bob with each capricious
gust. Cedar limbs thrash up and down
like green feather dusters. Right now,
weather is a lawless rogue with whip in hand,
black cape flapping wild. It is twilight
on the edge of frost, a hint of winter
with its blustery howls.

Shadows climb walls like phantom guests
who have come in uninvited. It is a night of
impoverished warmth, a time to pull a wingback
chair near fire and drowse within kindled light
while a blaze of logs releases a scribble of sparks.

## RAIN AND ENNUI

As if somebody walked off with the sun,
it rains all day, washing gutters clear,
weighing down last leaves.
I write from despair, watch out the window,
stare at monotony of water drops tracing
their signatures on glass.

I reread my poem, mostly shift in my chair,
gaze ahead, try to tell how rain evokes
melancholy, cramps the heart with sadness.
I want to blurt out what it means to be human
in a torn and lonely place.

To crush early evening dusk, I light the desk
lamp. Rain hammers casements. Seismic
thunder roars. I speak as a man
who has dragged himself into November,
daring to replace the spleen of desire with poetry.

PREPARING FOR WINTER

Red oak leaves, like many little deaths,
peel from limbs, curlicue to the ground.
Over and over, repetition of loss loosens
from each branch, settles upon the grass.
Sky is blue silk, and a flock of birds touch
amber sun with their wings.

I slump on a bench in Schiller Park, watch
enthusiastic walkers accumulate miles.
Landscapers rip out marigolds and begonias
as if they never mattered. Handfuls of fuchsia
fly to the flower heap. It appears as if
the world is being dismantled in preparation
for darker months.

Unafraid, geese gather on the walkway,
expect people to feed them. It feels wrong
I didn't bring bread or something. Minutes later,
they float on the pond out of reach.

A man and woman amble down the sidewalk
with their dog. I force myself to look at them.
I pretend I don't catch on to their romance as
I'm sad to be sitting on this bench by myself.

The geese suddenly return as if to collect
on a promise I can't keep. If they could talk,
I'd ask them if they are ever companionless
and what do they do on empty, winter nights?

# FAMILY AT THE LANCASTER FAIR

In mid-weight jacket, I mosey
under the gold of sun melted like butter
over yellow sugar maples. Dogwood flowers,
red as pomegranate. Each sassafras leaf
is a citrine gem.

Random people relax around picnic tables
in Rising Park. Loose leaves swallow
an occasional breeze, rolling across grass
like brittle, arthritic hands.

Two of my aunts and my parents follow
a path to the Lancaster Fairgrounds across
the street from the park, purchase powdered
elephant ears, amble among exhibits.

Dusk lights the red, old-fashioned Ferris-wheel
star from circumference to circumference.
I walk behind family as if framing them
in a memory photo. Neon lights from the
midway supplant surrounding leaf colors.
Family waits for me to catch up.
They are not far away as they will be
in a few years when death hands each of them
an irrefutable ultimatum. For now,
all roads lead to happy, and they have
no intention of turning back.

## AUTUMN EPISODE

I drive along route 50 in southern Ohio.
Autumn light, Holy light, washes
over my windshield like the saddest prayer.
Breeze across fields bends shifting grass.
Cracked-open milkweed pods show fuzzy,
white faces full of seeds. Acres of goldenrod
shine, a saffron sea. Edge to edge,
sky is sodalite blue.

I park alongside a field
of lupine, flax, coreopsis, and Shasta daisy.
Background foliage flaunts deep yellow,
flaming red, apricot orange
like the lower part of a candle flame.
Air is simply golden.

Thistles stick to my pant legs as I step
into the field closer to wildflowers.
If someone at that moment were to ask me
what is death? I would say it is
the absence of senses, deprivation of detail.
Compulsive urgency to share this perfect day
makes me want to cheat death, to open graves
and let those who lie in eternal dark be awake again
to leaves shiny as metal, hillsides that shimmer
in sunlight like variegated ends of kaleidoscopes.

I return to the car, a passing traveler stopped
for a while on the mortal road
of a temporary season.

**R. Nikolas Macioci** earned a PhD from The Ohio State University, and for thirty years taught for the Columbus City Schools. In addition to English, he taught Drama and developed a Writers Seminar for select students. OCTELA, the Ohio Council of Teachers of English, named Nik Macioci the best secondary English teacher in the state of Ohio. Nik is the author of fifteen books. Critics and judges called *Cafes of Childhood* a "beautifully harrowing account of child abuse," but not "sentimental" or "self-pitying," an "amazing book," and "a single unified whole." *Cafes of Childhood* was submitted for the Pulitzer Prize in 1992. In 2021, he was nominated for a Pushcart Prize and a Best of the

Net award. In 2022, he was nominated for a Pushcart Prize. More than two hundred of his poems have been published here and abroad in magazines and journals, including *Chiron, Concho River Review, The Bombay Review, Humana Obscura, and West Trade Review.* He won First Place in the 1987 National Writer's Union Poetry Competition, judged by Denise Levertov, First Place in The Baudelaire Award Competition, sponsored by The World Order of Narrative and Formalist Poets (1989), Second Place in *Zone 3's* first annual Rainmaker Awards, judged by Howard Nemerov (1989), and Second Place in the Writer's Digest annual competition, judged by Diane Wakoski (1991).

# BLACK DRAGON POETRY SOCIETY

# CERTIFIED AND APPROVED

www.ingramcontent.com/pod-product-compliance
Lightning Source LLC
Chambersburg PA
CBHW031513120626
46545CB00005B/1857